THE GOLFER'S
BUCKET LIST

THE GOLFER'S
BUCKET LIST

Golf courses you must play in your lifetime

CHRIS WHALES
DUNCAN CRUICKSHANK

NEW
HOLLAND

CONTENTS

INTRODUCTION

In this modern era of ready international travel and quality, yet affordable, resort accommodation, many ardent golfers are living the dream of playing the great golf courses of the world. What then are the golf courses every fan wants to play? Which of the world's great courses would constitute the golfer's bucket list … the golf courses you must play before you kick the (golf) bucket?

One thing all of these courses have in common is they condition a tradition of matching their sheer beauty with the harmony of their surroundings. Some of these courses were created by the Gary Player Design Company; others hold special memories through their playability, while many have left a lasting impression from famous tournaments.

Among this list are many of the great links of Scotland, England and Ireland as well as a selection of more recent 'link like' courses that borrow elements of links layouts; a wide variety of parkland style courses, from the classic layouts such as Augusta National and Royal Melbourne to modern creations in Europe, Asia and South Africa; the modern trend in resort courses and tournament specific courses in the USA; and spectacular layouts in California, USA, Indonesia and New Zealand. Lastly, because modern technology has allowed the creation of golf courses in previously inaccessible locations, a selection of desert courses from the United Arab Emirates, the bushveld of South Africa and the scenic Alps of Switzerland have also been included.

Selection and rankings of golf courses will always attract debate and controversy. The Golfer's Bucket List has tried to incorporate all the different types of courses – old and new, traditional and modern; built in a wide variety of settings, styles and geographic locations – to test the most ardent gold fanatic. One this is for certain … these are the golf courses you must play in your lifetime.

The Publisher

LEFT: Kauri Cliffs Golf Course in New Zealand.

Cape Kidnappers Golf Course, New Zealand.

GOLF COURSES
THE GREAT ARCHITECTS

Since golf's early days some 500 years ago the game has experienced several periods of evolution. Evidence of how it has grown over the centuries can be seen in the advances in equipment, particularly in the manufacture of the golf ball and the driver; the move in tournament format from matchplay to strokeplay; and changes in the character and appearance of golf courses.

The art of golf course architecture – a term first coined by renowned golfer and golf course architect Charles Blair MacDonald – has undergone an evolution of its own. While early golf courses were created by nature rather than an architect's hand and players found their own way from tee to green without the course dictating their strategy, modern courses are laid out by men who charge huge fees for both course design and construction.

While the identity of the first person actually to decide how a particular golf hole should look is lost in the misty origins of the game, it is recorded that the first group of people to dabble in golf course design were the early professional golfers. The most prominent of these was Old Tom Morris, a multiple winner of the Open Championship who lived at St Andrews where he ran a golf shop and acted as both professional and greenkeeper. Morris had a hand in the design of a number of classic layouts in the UK, including Muirfield in Scotland, Westward Ho! in England and Royal County Down in Ireland, a course deemed by many to be the finest venue for links golf in the world.

Morris popularized a course layout style that featured each nine returning to the clubhouse in a loop, as opposed to the first nine going out and the second nine coming back. To this day Morris's strategic layout at Muirfield remains one of the game's miracles of design. He laid out the first nine to play clockwise and the second nine to play anti-clockwise, thus ensuring that golfers experience the wind from every conceivable angle, and are thus tested to the full.

The 1920s were regarded as the golden age of golf course design and construction. It was during this period before the Great Depression that men such as Donald Ross, Alister Mackenzie, Harry Colt and AW Tillinghast produced some of their finest works.

Colt, the co-designer of Pine Valley in New Jersey, USA, led the revolution that saw golf course architecture move away from the notion that all but the perfectly struck shot should be penalized. He believed golf courses should test all shots in a player's arsenal, but that there was no need to severely punish all less-than-perfect shots.

Mackenzie, an English surgeon who served in the Boer War and World War I, created some of the game's most revered venues, including Royal Melbourne in Australia, Cypress Point and Augusta National in the USA, which he co-designed with Augusta National founder and legendary amateur golfer Bobby Jones. Together with contemporaries such as Tillinghast, whose designs include Winged Foot and Baltusrol, and Ross, who created Pinehurst No. 2 and many other great layouts, Colt and Mackenzie laid down the foundation of golf course architecture. The principles they established were so sound that they are still in use today, although in recent times there have been some changes to accommodate the need for multiple tees and irrigation systems.

Through the years after World War II, architects like Robert Trent Jones adhered diligently to the golden principles laid down by Colt and company. Others such as Tom Fazio, Pete Dye and professional golfers turned architects such as Jack Nicklaus, Gary Player, Arnold Palmer and Tom Weiskopf combined tried and tested design guidelines and principles with innovation, lifting golf course architecture to new heights with their spectacular creations.

LINKS GOLF COURSES
SHAPED BY THE HAND OF NATURE

Games similar to golf – like 'kolf', played in Holland, and 'chole', played in Belgium – existed in medieval Europe, but it is generally accepted that golf as we know it today originated on the 'linksland' of Scotland's east coast.

Linksland originally referred to the strips of sandy coastal land formed when the sea receded after the ice age. Over centuries, fine grasses and gorse bushes covered these undulating areas. Not suitable for agriculture, they were generally used as 'common ground' by the residents of nearby towns. Once golf became popular, golfers also ventured onto the linksland for their games. Today the word 'links' refers to coastal golf courses on which nature has dictated design and layout.

Despite varying opinions as to what defines a 'true' links course, several specific characteristics are generally found, although not all of these 'conditions' are essential. Certainly, many fine links courses, including some that have hosted the Open Championship, do not have all of them. Links courses are usually close to the sea, exposed to coastal winds. Design is dictated by nature since almost all were laid out before the advent of earth-moving machinery and landscape architecture. The subsoil tends to be sandy, while layouts typically wind their way through, over and around dunes covered with grasses and gorse bushes. The first nine holes usually head out from the clubhouse or starting point, while the second nine come back towards it – hence the terms 'outward' and 'inward nines'.

In the early days, golfers played to the same holes going out and coming back, but this became increasingly dangerous as the game grew in popularity, so it was decided to cut separate holes for the inbound nine. As a result, two holes were cut on the same putting surface, and 'double greens' were born. These are still featured on some courses today and many modern architects deliberately build one or two on new layouts to recreate a classic feel. The most famous are those at the Old Course, St Andrews, which has no fewer than seven.

Most of the world's links courses are on the coast of the UK and Ireland, although fine examples in other parts of the world include Paraparaumu in New Zealand and Humewood in South Africa.

Golf on links courses is very different to playing on parkland, desert or mountain courses. 'Links golf' demands a wide range of shots because of the vagaries of the weather, the undulating terrain, the fine strains of grass usually found on links courses and the firmness of the soil. Approach shots often have to be run to the pin by way of 'bump and run' shots, while deep bunkers are constructed of stacked soil bricks. Some, known as pot bunkers, are extremely small. (Well-known golf writer Bernard Darwin once wrote of a pot bunker: 'It has just enough room for one angry man and his mashie!') Water hazards are scarce on links courses but, when present, usually take the form of burns that run off to the sea. The most famous is the Swilcan Burn that runs in front of the 1st green at St Andrews.

LINKS-LIKE COURSES

The exhilaration offered by links golf has led today's golf course architects to replicate the characteristics of links courses in their designs. As the game of golf mushroomed across the globe during the course of the early 19th century, Scottish golf course architects spread the influence of links golf by incorporating links-like features into courses like Shinnecock Hills in the USA and Royal Melbourne in Australia. Modern architects like South African Gary Player have also used classic links features in layouts like the USA's Raspberry Falls and, more recently, The Links at Fancourt in South Africa.

Although these 'links-like' courses are often situated inland, golfers playing over the undulating fairways that wind between towering dunes find it hard to believe they are not close to the sea and that the layout is the work, not of nature, but of men with bulldozers and earth-moving machinery.

RIGHT: Turnberry golf course is built on a stretch of classic linksland on Scotland's Ayrshire coast. The green is protected by typical deep pot bunkers in the style of those found on the earliest courses, which were shaped naturally by sheep sheltering from the icy coastal winds.

PARKLAND GOLF COURSES
SHAPED BY MAN AND MACHINE

A natural progression in the evolution of the game was for golf courses eventually to move away from coastal linksland and be laid out on inland areas. Today, the vast majority of the world's golf courses are situated inland and most of these are 'parkland' in nature.

This descriptive term implies a course that has a park-like atmosphere, characterized by an abundance of trees, shrubbery and other attractive natural features such as lakes and streams. A key factor determining the status of a parkland course is its 'maturity' – tall trees lining the fairways, prominent water features and streams, and thick undergrowth alongside the playing corridor make the course appear established and 'mature'.

The secret of success on parkland courses is what is referred to in the golfing world as 'target' or 'dartboard' golf. While golfers will frequently run the ball along the ground to the green on links courses, approach shots on parkland courses are generally played through the air. And, while the greens on links courses are generally hard, those on parkland courses are often soft and receptive, meaning that a well-struck shot will stop quickly on impact. It is interesting to note that while most links courses have the same type of grass cover from tee to green, parkland courses generally have a variety of grasses, with Bermuda fairways and Bent grass greens being common species.

Because of the well-wooded nature of many parkland courses, longer shots often have to be 'shaped' through the air. It is less important to be able to hit the ball high or low in parkland environments, but the ability to draw or fade the ball is a major advantage.

Parkland courses can be classified into two broad categories: classical and modern. Older parkland courses, designed before World War II, are generally regarded as classics, while younger courses are referred to as modern layouts. In recent years, many classic layouts have been modernized through the reconstruction and enlargement of bunkers and greens. Close attention is paid, however, to preserving their classic characteristics and atmosphere. Modern parkland courses often have 'novelty' features such as railroad sleepers in bunkers and large water features specifically placed on the course to serve as hazards.

Given the fact that most of the world's courses fall into the parkland category, it comes as no surprise that the majority of high-profile golf tournaments are staged on parkland layouts. Although the British Open is played only on links courses, more Major championships have been decided on parkland layouts than on any other type.

The US Open is virtually always played on parkland layouts and even a course such as Pebble Beach, where Tiger Woods shattered a host of records during the 2000 event, has numerous parkland features and holes despite its status as an ocean course. Other notable parkland layouts that have hosted the US Open include Winged Foot in New York, Congressional in Washington, Oakmont in Pennsylvania and Pinehurst in North Carolina, while one of the most famous parkland layouts in the United Kingdom – Wentworth in England – has been home to the World Matchplay Championship for over three decades.

Two of the top three courses in the USA (as ranked by American publication Golfweek in 2000), Pine Valley and Augusta National, are parkland layouts, and Augusta's status as the home of the Masters has made it the world's most famous and televised golf course. Gary Player once commented: 'If there is a golf course in heaven, I hope it is like Augusta National. I just do not want an early tee time!'

RIGHT: Measuring 425m (465yd), the 5th hole at Oakland Hills is a long par four with typical parkland features such as lush fairways, tall trees and a stream crossing the playing area. This famous course has hosted the US Open Championship on no fewer than six occasions between 1924 and 1996, the year when American Steve Jones won his first Major with a four-round total of 278.

GOLF'S FINAL FRONTIERS
PUSHING THE BARRIERS OF NATURE

Modern earth-moving machinery and vast sums of money have allowed man to push aside nature's barriers and build golf courses in previously inhospitable environments. Desert, bushveld and mountain courses represent the breaching of golf's final frontier – a relatively new phenomenon because until recently it was impossible to build a golf course in an area without water, soil or trees, or on steep mountain slopes.

These classes of course are as much a triumph of advancing technology as they are of the skills and imagination of the golf course architects who
create them – not to mention the size of the bank balances that fund them.

Desert golf courses, in particular, are a triumph. Presenting golfers with wide open spaces, perfectly maintained courses, year-round sunshine and spectacular vistas from the dry yellows and browns of the desert backdrop, they create a striking contrast with emerald-green expanses of fairways and greens. Gary Player's Egyptian creation at Soma Bay, in addition to a number of courses that have sprung up in the United Arab Emirates – like the Emirates Golf Club which now hosts events on the European Tour – and American courses such as Mission Hills in Palm Springs, have helped to put desert golf on the world map.

Mountain courses, such as Crans-sur-Sierre in Switzerland, offer some of the most spectacular views in world golf – vistas that have not been lost on the golfing public through the televising of the European Masters played there every year.

Bushveld courses are unique to the continent of Africa. South African layouts such as the Gary Player Country Club and Lost City Country Club at Sun City near Johannesburg, as well as Leopard Creek near the Kruger National Park, are cut out of the rugged African bush. Leopard Creek, in particular, provides golfers with unparalleled close-up views of nature as wild animals freely roam the course. As golf has expanded around the world, golf course architects have been drawn by the spectacular views and variety of landscapes.

Ocean golf courses, such as Pebble Beach in California, are constructed on sites that cannot be classified as linksland although they are close to the sea, and they frequently contain elements of parkland courses when the layouts turn inland. When the layout runs close to the sea, however, they offer dramatic views and demanding shots, often played over high cliffs and crashing waves. Ocean courses, like links courses, are exposed to coastal winds that whip in off the sea and can instantly transform the character of the course.

A trend in modern golf course construction is towards 'stadium' courses – a phenomenon particularly popular in America. When designing these courses, the architects are at pains to create layout features that test golfers' skills, as well as to create enough space for spectators to view the action during big tournaments. As a result, high mounds are often found around tees and greens. Today, there are a number of TPCs (Tournament Players Courses) specifically designed to host professional events, including Gary Player's TPC at Jasna Polana in Princeton, New Jersey; the TPC at Sawgrass in Ponte Vedra Beach, Florida, which is the permanent home of the US PGA Tour's Players Championship; and the TPC at Summerlin, home of the Las Vegas Invitational.

While TPCs are designed specifically to host the world's best golfers under tournament conditions, resort courses are often designed with exactly the opposite in mind. They typically feature wide playing corridors, large greens and numerous tee options. Like TPCs, they are also a modern-day phenomenon, born out of the game's burgeoning popularity and the demand for playing facilities by golfers of all skill levels.

RIGHT: Switzerland's Crans-sur-Sierre is among the most scenic tournament venues used on the European PGA Tour, hosting the annual European Masters. Under snow for the winter months when the practice tee becomes a beginner's ski-slope, the course returns to peak condition for the summer golfing season.

PINE VALLEY

NEW JERSEY, USA

It was George Crump, owner of the Colonnades Hotel in Philadelphia, Pennsylvania, who first spotted the land on which Pine Valley now stands. An avid golfer, he used to travel from the Philadelphia Country Club to Atlantic City by train to play on a regular basis. On one such trip, he noticed the land he believed would be ideal for a golf course. He persuaded 18 of his fellow golfers each to part with US$1000 to purchase the 75ha (185 acres) of land covered with pine and oak trees, swamps and impenetrable bush.

Construction started in 1912, with Crump living in a small bungalow on site to oversee the felling of trees, laying out of fairways and construction of dams. With the assistance of Harry S Colt, the Briton who had designed Wentworth, Crump set about fulfilling his ambition of creating the most difficult course in the world.

Progress was slow. In 1918, with only 14 holes com-pleted, Crump died, having already spent someUS$250,000 of his own money to realize his dream. Fortunately, there was enough in his estate to call in Hugh Wilson, the creator of the Merion golf course in Philadelphia, Pennsylvania, and his brother Allen, to direct construction of the remaining four holes. The result would surely have pleased Crump and it drew praise from both course designers and players of all skills levels.

OPPOSITE: The approach shot to the par-four 13th is played along a fairway entirely flanked by sandy waste areas. Pine Valley is laid out on 74ha (184 acres) of forest and marshland on the highest piece of land in the region.

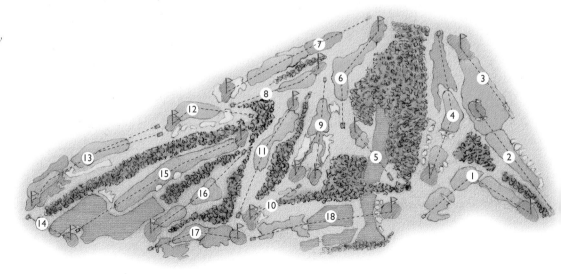

"*Pine valley fills you with dread and delight..It takes your breath away..its a monster..but its beautiful.*"

-Robert Trent Jones

Built on extremely sandy terrain, the Pine Valley course presents the ultimate challenge to golfers as they attempt to find the narrow strips of fairways dotted among vast, sandy waste areas.

With only two par fives – the 7th and the 545m (596yd) 15th – the par-70 course measures just over 6000m (6562yd).

Pine Valley's difficulty is legendary and there is said to be a standing bet among the members that newcomers to the course will never break 80 at their first attempt.

The great Arnold Palmer, about to be married and short of money, arrived to play at the course soon after triumphing in the 1954 US Amateur Championship. He took a number of bets that he would break 80 at his first attempt. Knowing he would be unable to pay if he lost, Palmer set about scoring a flawless 68 and left the course with a sizable wedding present.

Another well-documented story is of the late Woody Platt, who started with a birdie at the long par-four 1st with its inevitable drive over sandy wasteland. He then holed his 7-iron approach to the second for an eagle and holed-in-one at the short 3rd, which has nothing but 160m (175yd) of sand between the tee and green. At the 400m (437yd) par-four 4th, he birdied from 11m (36ft) and then returned to the nearby clubhouse at six under par after four to contemplate the rest of his round. Apparently, he took courage from a drink or two and never made it back onto the course.

Despite its fame, Pine Valley has never hosted a major championship, mostly because it cannot accommodate large crowds. The pinnacle of Pine Valley's exclusivity is showcased on the one day of the year it is open to the public: on the final round of the Crump Cup, an invitational tournament named after the founder of the club, for elite amateurs. Despite the lack of professional tournament hosting, Pine Valley is unanimously considered the best golf course in the world and was documented as such in Golf Magazine's Top 100 Courses In The World, as well as the best course in the United States in 2009 and 2011.

LEFT: The view from the tee of the 167m (184yd) par-three 14th, showing the shot that is played over water to a raised green.

RIGHT: The tee shot of the short par-four 8th is played across a large waste area known as the 'Sahara', towards the well-guarded green. The large grassy swale in the foreground alongside the green is an interesting variation on Pine Valley's extensive use of deep greenside bunkers as guarding hazards.

CYPRESS POINT

CALIFORNIA, USA

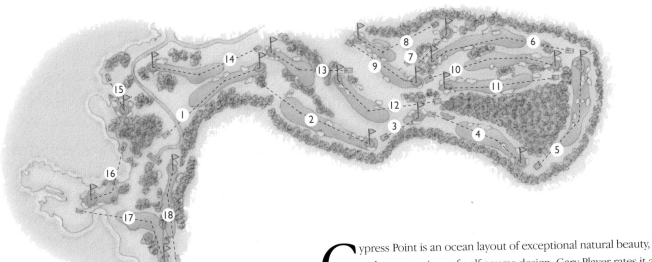

ABOVE: The view from the 16th tee. The hole is played into the prevailing wind to a green surrounded by bunkers. Many players use the alternative route to the left, playing a drive and a pitch and settling for a bogey four.

Cypress Point is an ocean layout of exceptional natural beauty, and a masterpiece of golf course design. Gary Player rates it as one of the world's most complete golf courses: 'Its terrain offers a hint of parkland that expands into a form of heathland and then a stretch of links by the sea, combining all forms of golf as we know it.'

Located 160km (100 miles) south of San Francisco, not far from its more famous neighbour, Pebble Beach, Cypress is situated in the foothills of the Santa Lucia mountains on the wild and rugged southern tip of the Monterey Peninsula. When the tide is out, the land drops in places some 20m (66ft) in a series of spectacular cliffs and, when the tide comes in, the huge waves of the Pacific Ocean pound the edge of the course.

Cypress Point is set within the Del Monte forest, and the fairways and some of the greens are lined with the inescapable, brooding presence of the huge Monterey Cypresses that give the course its name. Wild deer roam the peninsula, sea lions bask in the sunlight on the rocks and fishing boats dot the wide blue ocean.

ABOVE: The 15th, 16th and 17th holes at Cypress Point are played along the clifftops of the Monterey Peninsula overlooking the Pacific Ocean. In the foreground is the green of the par-three 16th, which requires a carry of 213m (233yd) over the ocean.

It was in this spectacular natural setting that famous golf course architect Dr Alister Mackenzie created his masterpiece in 1928. At no point was course quality sacrificed to take advantage of the natural beauty or majestic views, and the Scotsman built considerable slope and contour into the greens to compensate for the shortness of the course; it measures just 5965m (6524yd) from the championship tees. An unusual feature is the inclusion of both consecutive par fives and consecutive par threes. It also has all its par fives in the first 10 holes, and two par threes in the final four holes.

Undoubtedly the most spectacular hole on the course is the par-three 16th. The green and the tee are perched above the raging Pacific on either side of a cove, and the drive must carry the full 213m (233yd) over the water. Gary Player rates this as one of golf's most magical holes: 'The brave man bids for the green knowing full well the penalties of failure. His cautious opponent settles for a mid-iron along the clifftop with an outside hope of a chip and putt to save his par. It remains the classic example of strategic golf.'

When the hole is played into the teeth of the prevailing wind, it would be true to say that only the strongest of hitters can reach the green with an iron.

For many years, Cypress Point was one of the courses used for the Bing Crosby National Pro-Am (along with Pebble Beach and Spyglass Hill). It brought together movie stars and pop singers, sporting celebrities and politicians, as well as the tour stars. Neighbouring Poppy Hills has taken its place.

Despite its status, Cypress Point has never held a major championship and it remains one of the world's most exclusive golf clubs, with just 250 members. In 2011, it was rated #2 in Golf Magazine's Top 100 Golf Courses In The World.

BELOW: On the inland part of the course, the fairway of Cypress Point's par-four 11th is flanked by tall trees. Mackenzie's imaginative work here led to his being asked to collaborate with Bobby Jones on the creation of Augusta National.

PEBBLE BEACH

CALIFORNIA, USA

Punched out into the Pacific Ocean by the Santa Lucia Mountains on the south side of Monterey Bay, the Monterey Peninsula is home to three courses of the highest quality – Cypress Point, Spyglass Hill and Pebble Beach.

In 1914, Samuel Morse, nephew of the man who invented the telegraph, was sent to the Monterey Peninsula by the Southern Pacific Railroad Company to dispose of its real estate in the area. Recognizing the potential of the land, Morse bought some 2833ha (7000 acres) for US$1.3 million. Morse's company, Del Monte Property, sold the ground on which Cypress Point now stands for US$150,000. Convinced that a golf course would enhance the remaining land, he commissioned real-estate salesman Jack Neville to design and construct a golf course on part of it. Although not a golf course designer in the traditional sense, Neville was a fine golfer, having twice won the California State Championship, and it is difficult to believe that anyone could have bettered his design.

The opening holes run inland away from the sea, giving little hint of their later magic. The 3rd, a straightforward par four, runs west towards the sea and the next, a short par four, offers the first sight of the ocean.

Neville had wanted to build the par-three 5th hole along the clifftop, but Morse had sold that piece of land and the new owner could not be persuaded to sell. Only in 1997 did the Pebble Beach Company buy back the land and Jack Nicklaus was commissioned to design the new par-three 5th that now fronts the ocean as Neville had intended.

The par-four 8th rates as one of the most spectacular holes in world championship golf.

ABOVE: Tom Watson plays during the 1982 US Open at Pebble Beach. His triumph is best remembered for his chip-in birdie at the 17th to snatch victory from arch-rival Jack Nicklaus.

BELOW: Perched on the peninsula that forms one side of Stillwater Cove, the par-three 7th hole is typical of the dramatic clifftop layout of Pebble Beach.

"If I had only one more round to play, I would choose to play it at Pebble Beach. I've loved this course from the first time I saw it. It's possibly the best in the world." –

JACK NICKLAUS

At a length of 382m (418yd), it must be played carefully, driving along a plateau that borders the ocean. From there the second shot must be played over a ravine towards the green some 150m (164yd) away. Care must be taken not to hit the drive too far, which makes for a tough choice of club off the tee.

The 17th and 18th are among the most famous finishing holes in golf, with many dramatic tournaments being de-cided on these holes. One of the most well-known images of modern Major championships is that of Tom Watson sinking his chip shot for birdie in the 1982 US Open Championship. At 190m (208yd), the 17th is dangerously long, and is played to a narrow green that is exposed to all the winds that blow off the bay. The 18th is a dramatic par five that runs along the rugged coastline, doglegging slightly to the left. Despite his emphatic record-breaking 15-shot margin in the 2000 US Open played at Pebble Beach, even Tiger Woods managed to find the ocean with his tee shot in the second round. Former PGA and Open champion,and bad-boy of golf, big-hitting John Daly, managed to find a way to crash to a nine over par 14 on this closing hole in the second round, proof perhaps that even the better golfers in the world can be brought to their knees by this course.

Pebble Beach last hosted the U.S Open Championship in 2010, the year that marked 150 years of golfing majors. Those four days proved to live up to the hype surrounding the monumental anniversary with two aspects of the tournament cementing a place in golf history books. The first was Northern Irishmen Graeme McDowell, who in winning his maiden major became only the second Northern Irishmen to win golf major as well as ending a 40-year drought for Britain at the U.S Open.

In the same tournament, one of the game's greatest played in his last ever U.S Open. At the site of his 1982 U.S Open victory, legendary Tom Watson strolled down the 18th fairway clutching the hand of his son Michael as he wiped a tear away from his eyes and waved goodbye to America's national championship.

Although the $495 dollar green fee makes it the most expensive public golf course in the world, don't be deterred from playing the #1 public course in the US, Pebble Beach is a must play for every golfer.

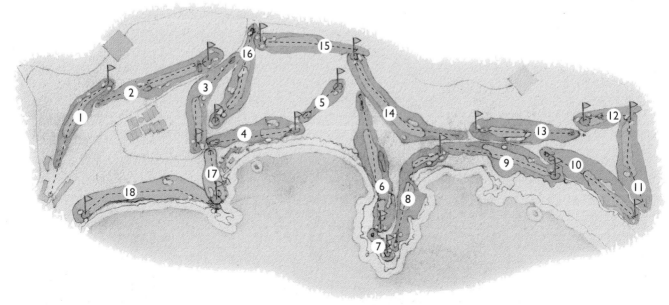

LEFT: Spectacular Pebble Beach. The 6th hole.

PHOTO CREDIT: Bernard Gagnon.

ST ANDREWS

FIFE, SCOTLAND

Golf has been played over the Old Course at St Andrews in Scotland for more than 450 years. While golf courses have spread and multiplied throughout the world since those early days, Mother Nature's creation on a windy peninsula jutting into the North Sea remains one of golf's true masterpieces. St Andrews is a mecca for golfing pilgrims, amateurs and professionals alike, and attracts thousands of visitors each year.

St Andrews is known as the home of golf, not only because of its long golfing history, but also because this barren piece of rolling scrub and heather, over which golf's pioneers first established the game, has evolved into one of the largest golfing complexes in Europe.

Today, the St Andrews Links Trust manages six golf courses, a 44-bay practice centre and a large and comfortable clubhouse. It is also home to the Royal & Ancient Golf Club of St Andrews (generally referred to as the R&A), which is recognized as the game's governing authority by all countries except the USA and Canada.

The term 'linksland' refers to the bleak and windswept strip of land 'linking' the ocean shore and the fertile farming regions further inland. Sheep grazed freely over these inhospitable areas of rolling dunes, grass and low bush, rubbing hollows – the forerunners of bunkers – into the side of the hummocks to seek shelter from the harsh sea winds. It was on this linksland that golf was first played at St Andrews, over courses shaped more by nature than by man.

In 1552, the burgh issued a charter giving Archbishop John Hamilton permission to establish a rabbit warren on the links at the town of St Andrews. The charter also confirmed the rights of the townspeople to play golf over the links – the piece of land today known as the Old Course.

Resembling a billhook when seen from the air, the shape of the course has not changed over the centuries, but its original 22 holes were reduced to 18 in 1764. This was one of the first changes brought in by the Royal & Ancient, which at that time had only been in existence for 10 years, but it was influential to the extent that 18 remains the standard number of holes for golf courses all over the world.

The Old Course is unusual in that it is set in the centre of St Andrews, with just a low white picket fence separating the course from the town itself. The early golf course layout style of nine holes out and nine holes back is preserved here, unlike modern courses which have two loops of nine holes.

The Old Course has a total of 112 bunkers, some of them notorious, like 'Hell' on the long 14th hole, 'Strath' on the short 11th, and the 'Road Hole Bunker', a particularly deep and steep-sided trap alongside the green of the par-four 17th 'Road Hole' that has ruined many a scorecard. This hole is unusual in that a road – off which the ball must be played – runs along the right side of the fairway and against the back edge of the green. Ben Crenshaw, USA Ryder Cup captain in 1999, once said: 'The Road Hole is the most difficult par four in the world because it is actually a par five.' Another interesting feature of the Old Course is its 'double greens', first introduced in 1856. Only the 1st, 9th, 17th and 18th holes have their own greens. The rest each have two holes cut in them and can be extremely large; it is not uncommon for a golfer to be faced with a putt of almost 100m (109yd), another quirk of this unique course and one that adds to its interest and enjoyment.

Tom Kidd won the first Open Championship to be held over the Old Course in 1873. This championship has been held here

RIGHT: One of the most famous views in golf: the bridge over the Swilcan Burn leading to the 18th hole of the Old Course at St Andrews, with the Royal & Ancient clubhouse in the background. The bridge was once a route into the ancient city of St Andrews.

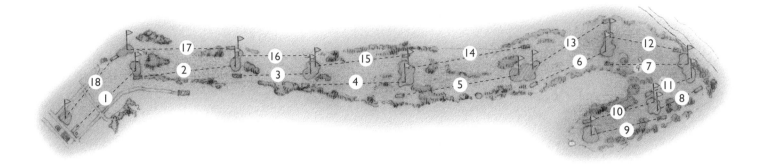

no fewer than 28 times, including the first Open of the new millennium. Golfers who have won the British Open at St Andrews – such as Bobby Jones, Sam Snead, Peter Thomson and Bobby Locke – have usually been at the peak of their careers at the time of their victory.

The greatest players of their age have always performed well here, Jack Nicklaus winning the Open in both 1970 and 1978, Seve Ballesteros in 1984, and Nick Faldo in 1990. Fittingly, it was at St Andrews that Tiger Woods became the fifth – and youngest – man to achieve the Grand Slam of Majors by winning the Open in 2000. Tiger continued his Open dominance at

St. Andrews in 2005with a fourteen under par total of 274.

The most recent British Open held at the Old Course in 2010 marked the 150th anniversary of golf's oldest major. In 150 years, the initial £ 10 shared prize had inflated to £ 850,000, which represented the transformation the sport of golf had taken. South African Louis Oosthuizen thrived on the significance of both the tournament and his home nation's Nelson Mandela day by finishing Sunday afternoon seven strokes clear of the field for his first major championship victory.

The Claret Jug will make its way back to 'the cradle of the game' in 2015 and is sure to be as dramatic as each Open at the Old Course.

LEFT Jack Nicklaus tees off in the final round of the 1978 Open Championship at St Andrews. He shot a 3-under-par 69 to win his third Open with a total score of 281.

AUGUSTA NATIONAL

GEORGIA, USA

Arguably the most famous and exclusive golf club in the USA, Augusta National was the brainchild of legendary amateur golfer Bobby Jones, who in 1930 uniquely won the Open and Amateur Championships of the USA and Britain.

Together with his friend and business associate, Clifford Roberts, Jones selected the land (then the Fruitlands Nurseries) on which he dreamt of building a top quality golf course of national renown. Despite the recent stock market crash and subsequent Depression, they found finance for their venture from wealthy businessmen who had survived the economic woes of the time. In 1933, some 80 founder members of Augusta National assembled, and Jones and Roberts were unanimously voted in as president and chairman respectively.

The course itself was designed by Dr Alister Mackenzie in consultation with Jones, and was formally opened in December 1932, just a month before the club was officially opened.

In 1934, the Masters tournament, originally known as the Augusta National Invitational Tournament, was first played here. It was not until the following year when Gene Sarazen hit the 'shot that was heard around the world' – the four-wood to score a two on the par-five 15th – that the tournament began to capture the imagination of the world's golfers. Since then the course that is famed for its absolute perfection in terms of conditioning has become the benchmark against which all parkland courses around the world are measured. The clubhouse, built in 1854 by the owner of the then indigo plantation, Dennis Redman, is considered to be the first cement construction in the southern USA. The 230m (250yd) drive up to the clubhouse, known as Magnolia Lane, is probably as famous as the course itself, boasting 60 magnolia trees planted in the late 1850s.

The course regularly undergoes slight design changes (or 'improvements', as the committee would have it) that include the growing of semi-rough and controversial lengthening. In 2001 Augusta's total length was 6329 (6925yd), but was extended to compensate for advancements in club and ball technology to its current length of 6800m (7445yd).

Each immaculate hole has a remarkable history, but it is possibly 'Amen Corner' (referring to holes 11, 12 and 13) that is most famous – the scene of many a change in fortunes come the Sunday of the Masters tournament. As the pressure of the final nine holes mounts, many a golfer has seen his dreams shattered as his ball finds the ubiquitous and notorious Rae's Creek.

ABOVE: Reconstructed in 1947, the par-three 16th at Augusta demands an accurate tee shot played entirely over water to the green, which slopes significantly from right to left.

ABOVE: Known as the Flowering Crab Apple, the long par-three 4th is often made difficult by deceptive wind, which makes it tough to reach the flag on the boomerang-shaped green.

Membership is strictly invitation-only and current members include prominent figures such as Bill Gates (founder of Microsoft), James D. Robinson III (former CEO of American Express) and Harold "Red" Poling (former CEO of the Ford Motor Company), to name a few. The history and exclusivity of the modern club combine to make this club #2 on the Golfer's Bucket List.

Augusta has hosted some of the most monumental occasions in golf history: Jack Nicklaus' last major championship victory and Tiger Woods' first, Ben Hogan's Masters win during his incredible year of 1953 and Tiger Woods' 'Tiger-Slam' in 2001. Arguably the most talked-about major championship shot of the last decade was played here; the famous Tiger Woods chip shot on the par 3 16th, which paused ever so dramatically on the lip before dropping to help Tiger claim the Green Jacket in 2005.

The 2012 US Masters proved to be just as dramatic as Woods chip in, with American Bubba Watson and South African Louis Oosthuizen tied on ten under par after the 72nd hole. Despite claiming only the fourth albatross in the history of the US Masters in regulation play, it was Bubba who hit the most memorable shot of the tournament on the 2nd playoff hole. Stuck behind a tree after a wayward tee shot, Bubba hit a specacular 140m (155yd) wedge shot that hooked some 36m (40yd) to rest just ten feet from the hole and an emotional Watson two putted to claim his first major and Green Jacket.

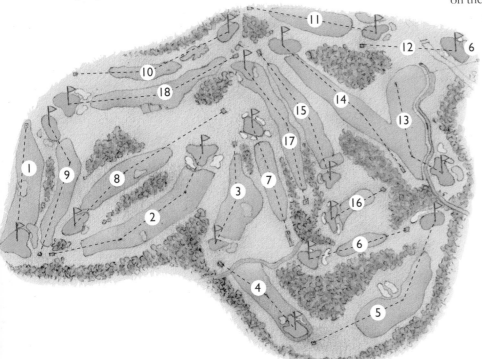

RIGHT: Before golfers hit the notorious Amen Corner at Augusta National, they play the 443m (485yd) 10th hole, one of the longest par fours in Major championship play. The 10th starts the second nine with a downhill drive from the tee situated near the clubhouse.

MUIRFIELD

EAST LOTHIAN, SCOTLAND

Although Muirfield has hosted the Open Championship no fewer than 14 times since the course was opened in 1891, the 88th Open in 1959 will always remain special to Gary Player. The 23-year-old Player opened badly, carding a 75 on day one, but improving slightly on day two with a 71 to make the cut by two strokes. Day three saw the young South African card a fighting 70 for a total of 217, four strokes behind the leaders, Britons Fred Bullock and Sam King, joining a group of 13 players on 217 or better.

After a promising start on the front nine on day four, where he shot a 34, Player seemed set to return an even better score on the back nine – a par on the par-four 18th would give him a 32 for a round of 66 and a realistic shot at the title. But Player hit his drive into one of Muirfield's many bunkers and then three-putted to drop two shots for a 68 and a total of 284.

Player left the 18th green in tears, believing he had let the Championship slip from his grasp. However, one by one, the leaders out on the course dropped away, with Bullock and Belgian Flory van Donck eventually finishing on 286. Player had just become the youngest Open Cham-pion since Willie Auchterlonie in 1893.

Muirfield is home to one of the world's oldest golf clubs, the Honourable Company of Edinburgh Golfers, formed in 1744 when 'several Gentlemen of Honour skilful in the ancient and healthful exercise of Golf' approached the Edinburgh City Council to donate a silver club as a prize for their annual competition on the Leith links. In later years, the exclusive club moved twice in search of less crowded golfing facilities, eventually settling in Gullane, along the coast east of Edinburgh where the present Muirfield course was laid out by Old Tom Morris and opened for play in 1891. Muirfield hosted the Open Championship the following year, the first time the event was played over 72 holes.

Since those early days, and due in some part to changes made by Harry Colt and Tom Simpson in the 1920s, Muirfield has evolved into one of the world's most re-spected championship courses. It has earned a reputation as one

ABOVE: The clubhouse at Muirfield overlooks the green of one of the toughest finishing holes in golf, the long par-four 18th.

LEFT: The green of Muirfield's par-three 13th hole is guarded by three fearsome bunkers. With more than 160 bunkers, many of them with steep turf walls, Muirfield is a private course and is home to the exclusive Honourable Company of Edinburgh Golfers.

of the fairest on the Open Championship roster, with few trees and no blind shots, hidden bunkers or water hazards. However, its extensive, deep bunkering (there are over 160 bunkers, many with walls of sod turf) and severe rough ensure a challenge worthy of the world's best golfers.

And the world's best have risen to the challenge over the years. The great Harry Vardon won at Muirfield in 1896, while James Braid won the Claret Jug here in both 1901 and 1906. Walter Hagen won his fourth and final Open on this course in 1929, while Henry Cotton won here in 1948 with a superb display of driving. In addition, American Jack Nicklaus recorded the first of his three Open victories at Muirfield in 1966 and went on to name his own course in Dublin, Ohio (USA), Muirfield Village after the Scottish course.

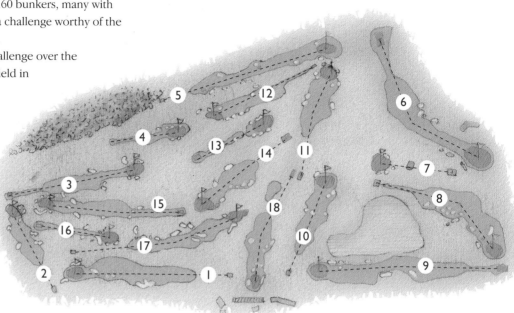

One of the most dramatic finishes in British Open golf came at Muirfield in 1972 when Mexican Lee Trevino chipped in from the rough for par on the par-five 17th. Briton Tony Jacklin, at that stage level with Trevino and well-positioned on the green for a birdie or par, was so shaken that he three-putted to hand Trevino the title.

The most recent hosting of a major championship by Muirfield was the British Open Championship in 2002, when Ernie Els emerged victorious out of a four-man playoff. On the fourth playoff hole, Els held his nerve and made par from a greenside bunker to lift the Claret Jug for the first time and capture his third major championship. The Senior British Open was also held here in 2007 and Tom Watson scored an even par 284 to claim victory.

While Muirfield's convenient location has seen it host many championship events, including the 1973 Ryder Cup, it is not a public course like the great links courses of St Andrews and Carnoustie. The exclusive Honourable Company of Edinburgh Golfers guards the course's privacy as jealously as it does the traditions of the game, ensuring the club's members play their golf on quiet and uncrowded fairways.

ROYAL COUNTY DOWN

NEWCASTLE, NORTHERN IRELAND

Situated in the coastal town of Newcastle, some 50km (30 miles) south of Belfast in Northern Ireland, the Royal County Down links course is considered by many to be one of the world's toughest. The course lies around the curve of Dundrum Bay and on a clear day the view stretches to the peak of Slieve Donard, the Isle of Man more than 60km (37 miles) to the east and, on the other side, the hills of Ballynahinch.

According to the minutes of the club, founded in March 1889, it was Old Tom Morris of St Andrews who, for the princely sum of four golden guineas, converted an existing nine holes largely created by nature and left recommendations for an additional nine.

The 6571m (7186yd) course has seen numerous changes during its many years of existence. In 1904, its professional, Seymour Dunn, suggested amendments, as did Harry Vardon in 1908. The last significant alterations were made by Harry Colt in 1926, but all who have worked on the course have preserved the very natural feel of this wonderful site, not least by retaining a number of blind shots.

Unlike many of the links courses which go out and back, Royal County Down has two nine-hole loops of entirely different character. This is thanks to George Combe, a founder member of the club who spent many years as chairman of the greens committee. The layout is   a traditionalist's paradise: down either side of the narrow fairways are high sand hills giving each hole a sense of   privacy and uniqueness.

The first three holes run northward along the beach that fringes Dundrum Bay, where the sand hills are thickly clad in grasping gorse and heather – meaning that off-target shots are easily lost. The battering winds off the Irish Sea present a complicating challenge since the sheer size of the dunes means that the ball is protected for parts of its flight, and exposed for others.

ABOVE: *Royal County Down is one of the few links courses that boasts spectacular scenery, as is evident here around the curve of Dundrum Bay. Although largely shaped by nature, the original course was laid out by Old Tom Morris in 1889.*

Another challenge is that as many as five tee shots are played blind towards aiming markers, and on a number of holes the approach to the green is at least partially obscured. An idiosyncratic feature of the bunkers is that they are fringed by reedy grass eyebrows, adding to their wild and fierce aspect and making an escape from them harder.

Three of the par threes are more than 183m (200yd) long, with bunkers, gorse and heavy rough that severely punishes any wayward shots. The long, 443m(486yd) par four 9th hole is one of the most popular photographs in all of golf, with the tee shot plummeting some 55m (60yd) down to a fairway that rises majestically up to the green.

The relative remoteness of Royal County Down has seen it stage only a few professional tournaments recently, most notably the 2000 Senior British Open won by Christy O'Connor Jr and the Walker Cup in 2007, where the United States defeated Great Britain and Ireland.

Despite the lack of tournament hosting, Royal County Down is widely regarded as one of the world's best-maintained golf courses and was rated #5 in Golf Magazine's Top 100 Courses In The World in 2011.

RIGHT: Although more than 180m (200yd) long, the par-three 4th is not the toughest of County Down's par threes – even though 10 penal bunkers await wayward shots. In the distance are Dundrum Bay and the Mountains of Mourne.

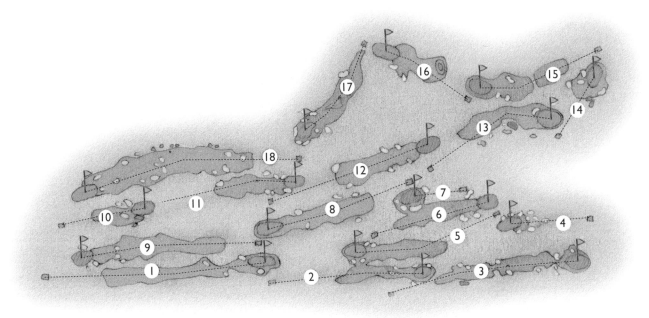

ROYAL MELBOURNE

MELBOURNE, AUSTRALIA

Royal Melbourne is one of the world's great championship courses outside the USA and the UK, an amalgamation of the work of two great golf course designers, Alex Russell and Dr Alister Mackenzie. The Royal Melbourne Golf Club was founded in 1891, a few years after golf spread to the southern hemisphere with the formation of Dunedin Golf Club in Otago, New Zealand, in 1871 and the Royal Cape Golf Club in Cape Town, South Africa, in 1885.

Membership of the Melbourne Club comprised many immigrants from the UK, some of whom hailed from the home of golf, St Andrews in Scotland. It was hardly surprising, then, that they sought out a stretch of heather-covered duneland very similar in appearance to Scottish linksland for the site of their new course in 1924. They imported a brilliant architect to design it, Alister Mackenzie, who had the wisdom to involve the current Australian Open champion, Alex Russell, as his partner in the design. Russell subsequently added a second course, and both courses were further refined by head green keeper, Claude Crockford, who deserves much of the credit for the lasting fame of Royal Melbourne. Holes from both courses make up the so-called Composite course, the selection partly governed by a road crossing. The result is a course of outstanding quality, with an intriguing mix of Augusta-like beauty and Scottish links-type characteristics. The course has earned a reputation for what are undoubtedly among the world's fastest and truest greens, while its rough-hewn bunkers add to the severity of the challenge it poses.

In 1959, Royal Melbourne hosted the World Cup (then called the Canada Cup). Appropriately, it was won by the home team of Peter Thomson and Kel Nagle. It hosted the event again in 1972 when the Taiwanese team was the surprise winner.

Although that a was major opportunity for Royal Melbourne, an even more prestigious opportunity would come in 1998 when the Presidents Cup, played between an American and an International team, was hosted here. It was the first time the event was staged outside of the US and the location proved to be crucial to the outcome; as the sweltering Melbourne heat aided the Internationals in their emphatic 20.5 to 11.5 victory.

The composite course at Royal Melbourne played host to the President's Cup again in 2011, after going through some significant changes in this interim period. Criticised as being far too short for professional golf, or 'Obsolete' as Greg Norman called it, the holes of composite course changed to a slower couch grass on the fairways to prevent excessive ball run, installed a fescue strip around each green to encourage running approach shots and returned to edging the bunkers by hand to achieve the natural feel of the landscape. The composite course was once again ready to host a President's Cup.

The President's Team, captained by Fred Couples, came into the tournament as favourites over the Internationals, who listed the legendary Greg Norman as captain. Over the four days between November 17 and 20, 34 matches determined the President's Team would win 19 to 15, with American Jim Furyk winning all 5 of his matches. In a stellar putting performance, Tiger Woods played his first 15 holes in 5 under par to clinch the winning point for the Americans.

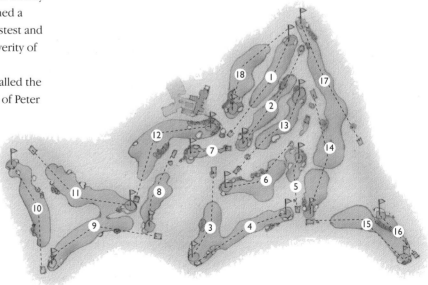

ABOVE: The majestic Royal Melbourne Golf Club encapsulates the character of Australian terrain and fluctuates in and out of the top ten golf courses in the world. Golf Magazine rated Royal Melbourne as #13 in its Top 100 Golf Courses In The World in 2011.

MERION EAST

PENNSYLVANIA, USA

"Acre for acre, it may be the best test of golf in the world"
Jack Nicklaus

When two of the greatest players in the history of the game give such generous reviews, one would not think that famous East course of Merion was designed by a Scottish immigrant with no course design credentials.

Thirty-two year-old Hugh Wilson was commissioned by the Merion Cricket Club, in 1910, to design a new golf course to be constructed in Haverford, Pennsylvania. As he had no experience in course architecture, Wilson took an extended trip back to Scotland and England to study the layouts of the top British links courses. Whilst records vary over the length of Wilson's working vacation, Merion historians state that Wilson cancelled his ticket on the *Titanic*'s only voyage for a few extra days of observation.

Those few extra days proved to be productive as several features of Merion's layout reflect the influence those courses had on Wilson; in particular the Scottish-style pot-bunkers, called the 'White Faces of Merion' and the famous 'Wicker-Baskets' that sit atop the pins in place of flags. It is believed Wilson borrowed the idea of the Wicker Baskets from shepherds he saw in England using them to store food away from the sheep, and add to the many challenges of Merion East as they give no indication of wind direction.

Of the four US Open Championships Merion has hosted (the fifth coming in 2013), the most memorable would be the 1971 U.S Open that resulted in Jack Nicklaus and Lee Trevino tied on Sunday afternoon, with the traditional the 18-hole playoff to follow on the Monday.

The day began with something you don't see in the modern game: an on-course prank. Trevino grabbed a toy snake out of his bag and threw over to a terrified Nicklaus, who scuttled off as the crowd chuckled. Whether nor not this affected Nicklaus' game, Trevino looked in control over the entire round, shooting a two-under 68 to Nicklaus' one-over 71 to claim his second U.S Open trophy.

Such an emphatic win prompted Trevino to declare his love for 'Merion'.

CAPTION: The approach shot into spectacular 11th hole leaves no room for error, with only some short rough to stop a wayward shot rolling down into the creek.

SHINNECOCK HILLS

LONG ISLAND, USA

The game of golf began its expansion from the remote coastal courses of Scotland to the far reaches of the earth in the early 19th century – first to England, then, following British explorers and colonizers, to India, New Zealand, Australia, mainland Europe, South Africa, South America and the USA. The first golf club in America was established in 1888. Situated at Yonkers on the east coast, it was appropriately called St Andrews. America's first 18-hole golf course, Shinnecock Hills, also on the east coast, opened in 1891 and, in 1896, it hosted the second ever US Open.

In the winter of 1889, William K Vanderbilt, son of the founder of the Vanderbilt empire, was visiting France where he met Scotsman Willie Dunn Jr, professional and course designer at Biarritz and former professional at Westward Ho! in England. Vanderbilt took a fancy to the game and, on returning to the USA, he began planning the construction of a golf course at the summer resort of Southampton on Long Island. Recruited to build the course, Dunn found the terrain to be ideal. Close to the Atlantic Ocean and exposed to the prevailing winds, with sandy, rolling hills and long, coarse grass, it resembled a piece of classic Scottish linksland.

With the help of 150 Native Americans from the Shinnecock tribe which occupied the far end of the island, Dunn completed 12 holes by 1891. A top architect of the time, Stanford White, was called in to build the stately clubhouse that still presides over the surrounding countryside today, and is the oldest in the USA.

In 1892, Dunn completed the remaining six holes, and the 18-hole layout quickly developed a large following among Southampton's wealthy summer residents, becoming the first golf club in the USA with a membership waiting list. In the early years, members played in red jackets in remembrance and imitation of the British tradition – to warn passers-by that golfers were present.

Although Shinnecock hosted the US Amateur and the US Open in 1896, and the US Women's Amateur in 1900, it measured only 4572m (5000yd) and was not considered long enough for championship golf.

In 1931, Dick Wilson expanded the layout to a championship length of 6349m (6944yd). Although this was considered relatively short at the time, the par-70 layout still utilized the effect of the prevailing southwest winds, with many par threes and short par fours playing into the teeth of the wind.

The course regained its Major status in 1986, hosting its second US Open a full 90 years after hosting its first Major. Although three players broke the course record of 68 by three strokes that year, they were tested by the narrow, undulating fairways bordered by long grass, and by the extensive bunkering. The event was won by American Ray Floyd with a score of one under par (279).

When American Corey Pavin won the 1995 US Open at Shinnecock, it was with a score of level par (280).

The layout was again extended prior the hosting of the 2004 US Open to its current length of 6397m (6996yd) and proved to be a worthy challenge for South African Retief Goosen, who won with a four under par total of 276.

Shinnecock Hill's opening hole, the par-four 1st, is named Westward Ho! after the course in England where Scottish designer Willie Dunn had served as a professional before going to the USA, but it is Shinnecock's par-four 18th hole that is perhaps most reminiscent of a Scottish links, with its undulating fairway and dense rough on either side. The wind from the right makes it difficult to keep the ball on the fairway and the long approach shot must clear the two bunkers guarding the front of the green. The hole provides a fitting close to a challenging and varied golf course.

In 2018 Shinnecock Hills will host its fifth US Open Championship, leaving the professionals curious as to what changes the layout might employ.

Shinnecock Hills Club House.

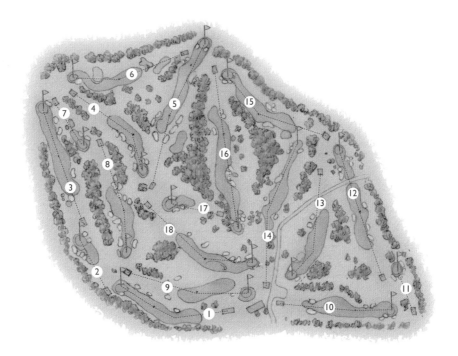

LEFT: The approach shot into spectacular 11th hole leaves no room for error, with only some short rough to stop a wayward shot rolling down into the creek.

ROYAL DORNOCH

HIGHLAND, SCOTLAND

In the far northeast corner of Scotland, just eight degrees outside the Arctic Circle, Royal Dornoch takes one back to the misty origins of the game of golf. A course of exceptional quality and wild beauty, it has been excluded from the Open Championship roster only because of its remoteness.

Although the club itself was not founded until 1877, records show that golf has been played over this piece of barren linksland since the early 1600s; only St Andrews and Leith can claim to be older. The course remained relatively unknown until the 1960s when American golf writer Herbert Warren Wind described it in glowing terms, and it has since been visited by such top players as Gary Player, Ben Crenshaw, Tom Watson and Greg Norman.

The 6124m (6697yd) par-70 course follows the traditional layout style of nine holes out from the clubhouse and nine holes in. The first eight holes hug the inland edge of the coastline, winding through thick gorse between old dune embankments. The remaining 10 holes are played back along the coast of the Dornoch Firth, skirting the sandy beaches and exposing golfers to the full force of the stiff prevailing west wind. The course is characterized by deep pot bunkers and raised greens with fall-aways on either side that punish the errant shot.

Although Dornoch takes one back to the era of natural courses when major landscaping and reconstruction were not possible and the course was determined by the lie of the land, the layout has, at various stages in its past, been shaped by some of the most influential men in the history of the game. Royal Dornoch

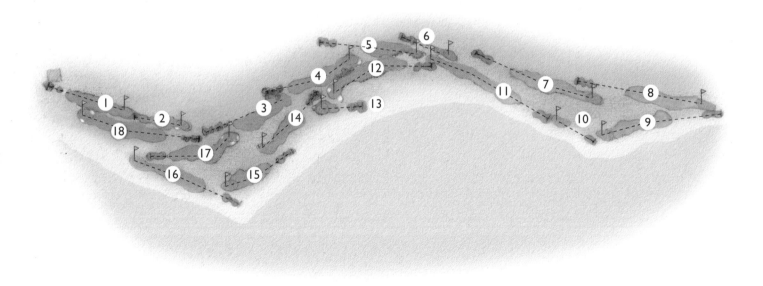

ABOVE: The layout at Royal Dornoch hugs the coast of Dornoch Firth, exposing golfers to the force of the strong westerly wind, particularly on the back nine.

was originally a nine-hole course, but after 10 years Old Tom Morris was called in from St Andrews to add a further nine holes.

However, it was one of the pioneers of greenkeeping and course maintenance, and the most prominent man
in Scottish golf at the time, who most shaped the development of the course – in 1883, Scotsman John Sutherland was appointed secretary of the club, a position he held for 50 years, and together with JH Taylor, he made several revisions to the layout. Donald Ross, the club's early greenkeeper, departed for the USA at the beginning of the new century and went on to become one of the game's greatest course architects, basing the design of many courses in the USA on Royal Dornoch – Pinehurst No. 2 being one of the best-known examples. Ross was also involved in the design of Seminole and Oakland Hills in the USA.

The first tee of the course is a stone's throw from the centre of the town of Dornoch, a cultured village just over 300km (188 miles) north of Edinburgh. Although Dornoch's remoteness ensures that its solitude will never be disrupted by the hustle and bustle of professional championship golf, the course was rated #3 in Golf Digest's Top 100 Courses Outside the U.S in2007and the combination of classic links golf and fine scenery continues to attract a steady stream of golfing pilgrims.

Tom Watson summed it up best when he said: 'This
is the most fun I've had playing golf in my whole life.'
And he's played some.

LEFT: The thick gorse covering the dune embankments at Royal Dornoch is attractive in full bloom, but provides a formidable hazard to golfers. Situated in a remote corner of northeast Scotland, this historic links is a course for the avid traditionalist.

BALLYBUNION

COUNTY KERRY, IRELAND

"Ballybunion is a course on which many golf architects should live and play before they build courses. I consider it a true test of golf"

-Tom Watson

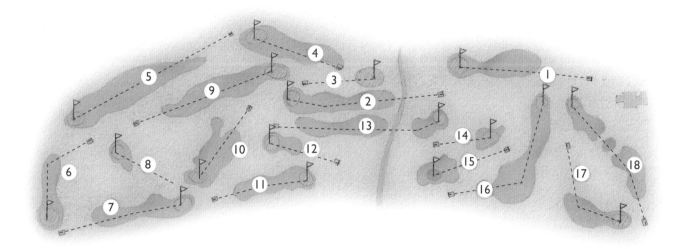

D eep in the county of Kerry in the southwest corner of Ireland, Ballybunion is reputed to be one of the finest links courses anywhere in the world. Because of its remoteness, it has rarely hosted professional tournaments, so there was much rejoicing when the Murphy's Irish Open was held there in 2000, Sweden's Patrik Sjöland taking the title with a 14-under-par total.

The club had a difficult start. Founded in 1893, it soon found itself in severe financial difficulty and it was only five years later that retired Indian Army
officer Colonel Bartholomew came to its rescue. He commissioned Lionel Hewson to lay out the first nine holes, but it was not until 1927 that the remaining nine holes were constructed and the course became a full 18-hole championship facility.

The 1st hole is a relatively simple opener with a drive to a wide

fairway running downhill. Thereafter, things soon become more testing. The bunkers in the fairway of the 2nd hole make par almost impossible if found with the tee shot, while the third is a long par three played to a severely undulating green. The 7th and 8th holes are played along the clifftops which, while affording astounding views of the Atlantic Ocean, are open to mighty winds that whip off the sea. The remainder of the course meanders through sand dunes, with a small stream fronting the green of the relatively short par-five 13th. The 17th boasts possibly the course's most spectacular tee shot, played from high up with dunes on either side.

When a new clubhouse was built in 1971, the order of the holes was changed to start at what had been the 14th hole. The bunker on that hole is still known as Mrs Simpson, named after the wife of the course architect, Tom Simpson, who tinkered with the course layout shortly before the 1937 Irish Men's Closed Championship. Simpson kept his changes to a minimum, re-siting just three greens and constructing his controversial bunker, which is placed in the middle of the fairway in the driving area.

In the late 1970s, 'Friends of Ballybunion', under the leadership of Jackie Hourigan, raised over £100,000 to save Ballybunion's cliff faces from erosion.

Recently, the Old Course at Ballybunion was ranked #17 in Golf Magazine's Top 100 Courses In The World in 2011 as well as #3 in Golf World Magazine's Top 100 Irish Courses.

LEFT: The tee shot on the doglegging par-five 16th must find the fairway that runs perpendicularly and slopes upwards from the Atlantic Ocean. The green is protected by two deep bunkers on the right as players approach it.

RIGHT: Ballybunion's 17th, a mid-length par four played alongside the ocean, curves past a high dune to an angled green.

Oakmont

PENNSYLVANIA, USA

"It's really a neat, special place."
-Phil Mickelson

The Oakmont Country Club in Oakmont, Pennsylvania, was the brainchild of its first president Henry C Fownes, a local steel magnate who decided to build a brutally tough course that would bring even the best players to their knees. In 1904, with 150 men and 25 mule-teams, he completed the first 12 holes in just six weeks, while the remaining six were added in spring later that year.

The course, built on a stretch of flatlands in the foothills of the Alleghenies, opened with a par of 80, including a total of 220 bunkers and no fewer than eight par fives, as well as a par six. Within a year Fownes, who is said to have had a bunker fixation, added another 130, bringing the total to an unprecedented 350.

Two bunkers in particular have become legendary in world golf, namely the 'Sahara' on the 8th and the 'Church Pews' which separates the 3rd and 4th fairways. The Sahara bunker – some 73m (80yd) long and 32m (35yd) wide – reputedly took 11 truckloads of sand to fill, while the 55x37m (60x40yd) Church Pews bunker is distinguished by seven grassy ridges that run across its length.

Although bunkers may dominate the course, it is the punishing greens that visitors remember most vividly. In the US Opens of 1927 and 1935, the winners – the Silver Scot, Tommy Armour, and Sam Parks, a local golfer who knew the course exceptionally well –

RIGHT: Sand everywhere you look. . . the par-four 14th requires an accurate drive threaded between the numerous bunkers on each side of the fairway. Once on the putting surface, the exceptional speed of the Oakmont greens provides a further challenge.

FAR RIGHT: The infamous Church Pews bunker lies between the 3rd and 4th holes, threatening the tee shots on both.

scored 301 and 299, respectively. Considering that par was 288, this clearly indicates how the brutal course could make a mockery of even the best players.

Following World War II, it was agreed to make Oakmont less intimidating, so the unusually narrow fairways were widened and the number of bunkers was sub-sequently reduced to under 200.

Oakmont Club has long been known for doing things its own way and the US Opens of 1953 and 1962 were marred by disagreements with the US Golf Association over the rakes used to smooth the bunkers. The unique rakes left deep furrows in the sand into which trapped balls would roll – proving nearly impossible to extricate successfully. Controversy broke out again in 1983 when the players in the US Open were greeted by rough that was 23cm (9in) thick in places, meaning that anyone who missed the fairway had to hack at the ball just to get it back on to the fairway.

Given all these disagreements it is perhaps strange that Oakmont has hosted eight US Open Championships, a national record. All were won by star American professionals like Ben Hogan and Jack

Nicklaus – until 1994, when South Africa's Ernie Els triumphed in a three-way playoff against Loren Roberts and Colin Montgomerie.

Thirteen years later, the international domination continued at Oakmont when Argentine Angel Cabrera shot a 5 over par 285 to claim the 2007 US Open from Tiger Woods and Jim Furyk, by a single shot.

Cabrera's win was regarded as one of the toughest US Open tournaments in history, as preparation for 2007 included deepening the bunkers and removing nearly 5000 trees planted during the 1960s to restore its original links style. Only eight rounds were played under par during the tournament, Cabrera's Thursday and Sunday scores of 69 (-1) were two of them.

Recently, the testing 6,634 m (7,255 yd) layout hosted the 2010 US Women's Open, won by Paula Creamer, and will host the US Open again in 2016. It was also ranked #8 in Golf Magazine's Top 100 Courses In The World in 2011.

Oakmont is the only golf course in the USA to have been declared a National Landmark, an honour bestowed in 1987.

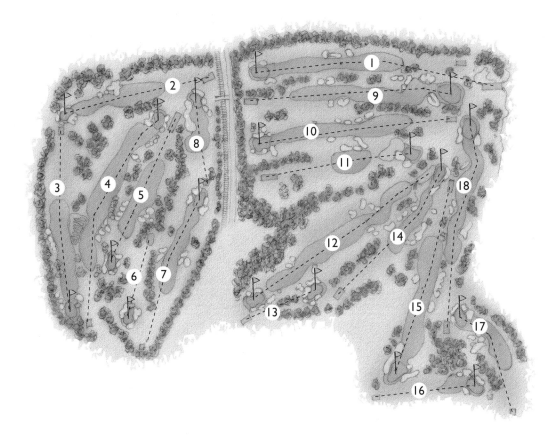

PINEHURST

NORTH CAROLINA, USA

"Proving the adage that everything old is new again, Pinehurst Number Two has roared onto the Must-Play list of any passionate golfer and is now nothing less than the best inland public course in North America."
-Larry Olmsted, Forbes.com

The Pinehurst story began late in the 19th century when Boston manufacturer, James Tufts, purchased 2023ha (5000 acres) of land in the Sandhills region of North Carolina with a view to developing a hotel and leisure resort that would offer wealthy East Coast residents an escape from bitter northern winters. Soon recognizing the need for golfing facilities, Tufts had an 18-hole layout built by an amateur course designer. Later named Pinehurst No. 1, this course was opened in 1898.

The Tufts family had previously met a young Scottish professional-greenkeeper, Donald Ross, at Dornoch. In 1898 Ross emigrated to work at Oakley Country Club in Massachusetts, where, once again he caught the eye of the Tufts. He was soon invited to become winter golf professional at the new resort. After redesigning Pinehurst
No. 1, he began work on what was to become a masterpiece of golf course architecture, Pinehurst No. 2. Although he went on to build, design or redesign over 400 golf courses throughout North America – including two other courses at Pinehurst and several more in the region – Pinehurst No. 2 is regarded by many as Ross's best work.

Drawing on his Scottish heritage, Ross introduced mounding, extensive bunkering and raised, contoured greens to the barren piece of land to create a layout that is demanding yet fair. Although generally large, the greens are convex, causing any inaccurate or misdirected shot to roll off into the surrounding collection areas. Once the golfer is on the green, the subtle slopes demand a deft touch with the putter.

For the 1999 US Open the course measured 6561m (7175yd), playing to a tough par of 70, and, with Donald Ross's raised greens

ABOVE: Pinehurst No. 2 hosted the 1994 US Senior Open. This view of the par-five 16th shows the course's only water feature, which requires a carry of 165m (180yd) off the tee.

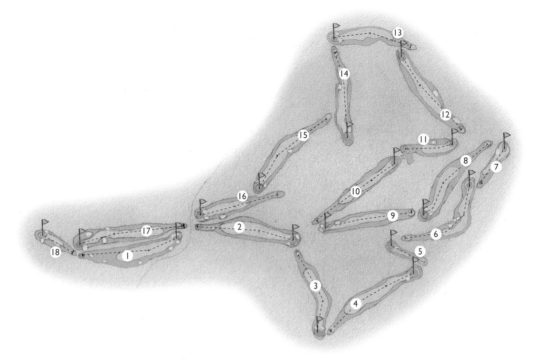

protected by collars of thick rough, scoring was high. Normally the fairway landing areas are generous, and the bunkers – numbering 109 in all – and greens are generally visible from the tees. Although the exhausted timberland on which Ross laid out the course was relatively open at the time, the pines that gave the area its name have grown thick and tall. Today, they line each fairway, creating a wonderful atmosphere of solitude and tranquillity.

Pinehurst's relative inaccessibility has meant that its No. 2 course has hosted fewer championship golf events than befits a layout of its stature. In 1936, it hosted its first Major, the US PGA Championship, but it was 63 years before the course returned to the Major roster when Payne Stewart held off Phil Mickelson to win his second US Open title in 1999.

The US Open returned to Pinehurst six years later when in 2005, New Zealand's Michael Campbell came from four strokes behind Sunday's leader to claim the trophy by two shots from a charging Tiger Woods.

In other prestigious tournaments, the course also hosted the 1951 Ryder Cup, the 1991 Tour Championship and the 1994 US Senior Open.

Pinehurst has always maintained strong links with the amateur game, as the 1962 and 2008 US Amateur Championships were staged here. Pinehurst No. 1 hosted the annual North and South Amateur Championship from 1901 to 1908, after which it moved to Pinehurst No. 2, which has been its home ever since. Richard S Tufts, the grandson of Pinehurst's founding father, made a major contribution to the development of the game in the USA, and was also one of the founders of the World Amateur Team Championship. Now known as the Eisenhower Trophy, it is regarded as the world's most prestigious amateur team golf tournament.

Pinehurst No. 2 may have hosted few great events, but it has produced several great champions. Ben Hogan won his first professional title here in 1940, Jack Nicklaus won the North and South in 1959, and Walter Hagen won the event on three occasions. The incomparable Babe Zaharias triumphed in the North and South Women's Amateur in 1947. Other worthy Pinehurst champions whose photographs line the corridors of the stately clubhouse are Jack Nicklaus's son, Jack Nicklaus II, Curtis Strange, Corey Pavin, Billy Andrade and Davis Love III.

Major changes were made to the course in 2010 and by March 2011, Pinehurst No.2 had increased the width of the fairways and eliminated all forms of rough from the course. A total of 35 acres of rough were removed and replaced with sand, wire grass and pine straw to restore the native landscape.

The fairways were made firmer to increase roll and reward shots that follow the contours of the fairway whilst punishing shots that do not. The bunkers were also given a 'natural' facelift to restore the look of the 1940s layout and will certainly test the world's elite when Pinehurst No.2 hosts the US Open in 2014.

Today, the Pinehurst Resort and Country Club is America's premier golf resort and many of the world's rich and famous have holidayed at Pinehurst over the past 100 or so years, including Bing Crosby, Michael Jordan, Oprah Winfrey, the Rockefellers and the DuPonts, while Amelia Earhart actually landed her plane at the resort's airstrip.

ABOVE: The 17th hole at Pinehurst No. 2 is a par-three of 174m (190yd) played through a grove of tall pines. Typical of the putting surfaces at Pinehurst, the green is slightly raised, directing wayward balls into the large bunkers on either side.

ROYAL PORTRUSH

ANTRIM, NORTHERN IRELAND

Royal Portrush, situated in Portrush, County Antrim, is one of three royal courses in Northern Ireland. The club was founded in May 1888 by Colonel JM McCalmont and JS Alexander, known as the Admiral of Portlenone. Five years later, the club was granted royal patronage by the Duke of York and became the Royal Portrush Golf Club, with the Prince of Wales (later King Edward VII) as patron. The earliest and most famous course lies near the ruins of its namesake, Dunluce Castle. The first nine holes were laid out in 1888 with another nine being added the following year. Back then, eight holes were laid out on the land side of the coastal road that leads to the famous rock formations of the Giant's Causeway but, over the years, substantial changes have seen the course move further out into the dunes towards the sea. From the highest point of these dunes the player catches glimpses of the hills of Donegal in the west, the Isle of Islay and the Southern Hebrides in the north, and the Giant's Causeway and the Skerries to the east.

Dunluce's fairways are extremely narrow, with all holes except the 1st and 18th doglegging fairly severely one way or the other. Although the spectacular green of the par-four 5th 'hangs' on the edge of a cliff, it is the par-three 14th that is probably Ireland's most famous. Depending on the wind, its 192m (210yd) can require anything from a medium-iron to a well-struck driver to reach the putting surface, which features a chasm to its right – giving the hole its well-deserved name of 'Calamity Corner'.

In 1951, Royal Portrush hosted the Open Championship – the only Irish course to have been afforded this singular honour – with Max Faulkner taking the title. The course record of 66 around the 6108m (6680yd) par-73 layout was set in the same year by Jack Hargreaves.

The 6531m (7143yd) layout also enjoyed some recent exposure when it hosted the 2012 Irish Open, which was the first time Northern Ireland had hosted a European Tour event and the first time the country had hosted the Irish Open since 1953. Northern Ireland's success in major championships, with ambassadors Darren Clarke, Graeme McDowell and Rory McIlroy all enjoying recent victories, has inspired the R&A to announce a possible hosting of the British Open at Royal Portrush in the future.

ABOVE: *The par-three 14th, one of the most famous holes in Ireland, is known as Calamity Corner. Here the tee shot demands anything from a medium-iron to a driver, depending on the wind.*

LEFT: *From the fairway of Royal Portrush's par-five 2nd, the town of Portrush in County Antrim can be seen in the background. The course has hosted the Open Championship on one occasion, when England's Max Faulkner won his only Open title.*

OAKLAND HILLS

MICHIGAN, USA

"The greatest test of golf I have ever played, and the toughest course."
-Ben Hogan

In 1916, the dusty Maple Road in southeastern Oakland was almost a day's journey from the heartland of the US motor industry in Detroit. Undeterred by the distance, two golf enthusiasts decided to transform 400ha (988 acres) of rolling farmland lining Maple Road into a golf course. The men were Norval Hawkins, who had become Henry Ford's first accountant in 1903 and later the company's first sales manager, and Joseph Mack, who handled printing and advertising for the Ford Motor Company. On 17 June 1916, they met 46 golf-loving friends and acquaintances at the Detroit Athletic Club for the first board meeting of the Oakland Hills Country Club. The club's first members, numbering 140, each paid US$250 to join.

To design the course, the board hired famous Scottish golf course architect, Donald Ross, who had designed Royal Dornoch in Scotland and over 100 courses in the USA. Ross also later built the Scottish links-style North course on the other side of Maple Road. 'The Lord in-tended this to be a golf course!' Ross exclaimed when he first saw the landscape.

In 1917, architect C Howard Crane submitted the plan for a clubhouse modelled on George Washington's Mt Vernon home, an imposing building that still stands today. The course – a par-72 layout measuring 6450m (7108yd) from the back tees – opened the following year, when Walter Hagen was appointed as the first pro, working out of a chicken coop alongside the first hole.

Oakland Hills has hosted six US Open Championships, dating back to 1924 when Bobby Jones was upset by Cyril Walker, as well as two US PGA Championships and two US Senior Opens. Prior to the 1951 US Open, the US Golf Association called on renowned English-born course architect Robert Trent Jones Snr to modernize the

ABOVE: The 16th at Oakland Hills is a dogleg right par four played alongside a large lake. In the 1972 US PGA Championship, Gary Player played his second shot over the trees and lake onto the green, from where he made a remarkable birdie.

Oakland Hills South course. His modified layout raised more than a few eyebrows from the field that year. The fairways were narrower – some just 23m (25yd) wide – and the rough was punishing. There were also 120 bunkers strategically positioned to guard the fairway landing areas and the greens, which were also surrounded by wide, deep sand traps, many with overhanging lips. The last five holes of the course were particularly demanding and became known as the 'Fearsome Fivesome'.

American Ben Hogan came to Oakland Hills that year as the US Open defending champion. Working relentlessly at mastering the brutal layout, he steadily reduced his scores over the first three days, carding 76, 73 and 71 to go into the final round two strokes behind joint leaders Bobby Locke and Jimmy Demaret. Until then, no one had scored below 70 in the event, but Hogan proceeded to play what has come to be recognized as one of the best rounds of championship golf ever. His 67 gave him a comfortable victory over Clayton Heafner, whose 69 was the only other score to break 70. After the event, Hogan commented: 'I'm glad I brought this course, this monster, to its knees.'

The 1950s also brought other changes to Oakland Hills. Golf carts were introduced for the first time and the men's locker room was air-conditioned, although the ladies' locker room in the basement remained hot and muggy in the summer. It was not until 1975 that a bridge over Maple Road was built to connect the two courses and the ladies moved out of the basement into their own dressing room above ground.

Although at times in its history Oakland Hills had to advertise for members, today it has a waiting list of two-and-a-half years and the initiation fee is a princely US$48,000.

Firmly entrenched on the championship roster, the 6808m (7445yd) South Course has hosted some spectacular moments of golfing history in the last eight years, beginning with the 2002 US Amateur, won by Ricky Barnes.

In 2004, Oakland Hills played host to the prestigious Ryder Cup, the team competition held between Europe and the United States. This was the 35th edition of the tournament and saw the Europeans beat USA 18.5 to 9.5 points, the largest winning margin of the European team in the history of the event.

Four years later, Europeans continued their formidable record at Oakland when Ireland's Padraig Harrington won the 2008 PGA Championship by two strokes. A monumental occasion for Harrington, the victory was his second consecutive major of the year and marked the first European-born winner of the PGA Championship in 78 years, as well as the first Irish winner of the tournament ever.

Detroit has expanded considerably since the early days of the 20th century when Oakland Hills was established by Hawkins, Mack and their friends. Today, the course lies in the suburbs on the outskirts of the city. Although not a scenic layout in the mould of Augusta or Pebble Beach, it is a formidable golf course that forms a worthy challenge for the world's best golfers in the new millennium, and will test elite amateurs when it hosts the 2016 US Amateur.

RIGHT: The slightly elevated green of the par-four 6th hole at Oakland Hills is surrounded by bunkers and tall trees. Laid out in 1917, the course is situated on a piece of land that architect Donald Ross claimed 'the Lord had intended to be a golf course'.

TURNBERRY

AYRSHIRE, SCOTLAND

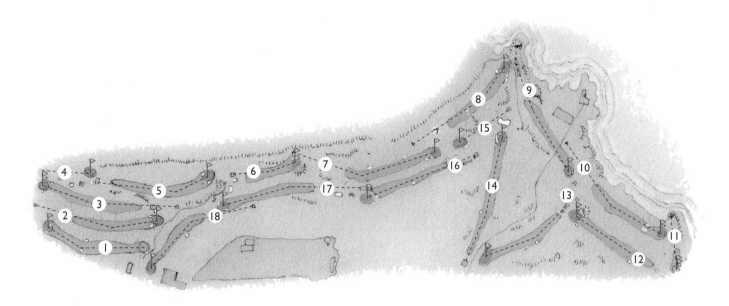

At the southernmost end of a stretch of classic linksland on Scotland's Ayrshire coast lies Turnberry, the site of one of the world's most beautiful and challenging golf courses. High on a hill overlooking Turnberry's Ailsa course is the famous Turnberry Hotel. Looming from the Firth of Clyde behind the links is the stark silhouette of Ailsa Craig, a huge round island of granite, while the Isle of Arran and the Mull of Kintyre can be seen beyond.

Turnberry has a long and eventful past and has, in recent years, been the scene of dramatic golfing moments in its short championship history. The third Marquis of Ailsa leased the land at Turnberry to the Glasgow and South Western Railway Company, and 1883 Open champion Willie Fernie, then the professional at nearby Troon, finished designing two 13-hole courses on the site in 1905. The Turnberry Hotel was built at the same time.

Turnberry's rise to championship status was delayed when, during World War I, the Royal Flying Corps built a training airfield on the site. Although the course was restored after the war – when a second layout, the Arran course, was also built – it was again severely damaged during World War II when the Royal Air Force built an airfield over the courses. Thanks to the efforts of Frank Hole and McKenzie Ross, the course was rebuilt and restored to its former glory in the years following the war. Remnants of the airfields can still be seen

"Turnberry is as close to Heaven as we golfers get."
-Tom Watson

ABOVE: The lighthouse at Turnberry stands on a rocky headland jutting into the Firth of Clyde. It was built in 1873 by Robert Louis Stevenson's father, a renowned engineer.

on the course, and a monument to the 119 airmen who died while stationed at Turnberry during the two wars stands beside the 12th green.

Soon after its restoration, Turnberry was awardedchampionship status, hosting the Scottish Championships and the News of the World Matchplay in the 1950s, as well as the Amateur Championship in 1961. It was some years, however, before it was included on the Open roster. It hosted its first Open in 1977, which saw one of the most dramatic head-to-head battles in championship golf.

Known as the 'Duel in the Sun', it was a battle between Americans Jack Nicklaus, aged 37, and Tom Watson, aged 27, fighting for the Claret Jug and the position of number one golfer in the world. Nicklaus, the master, and Watson, the pretender to the throne, matched each
other shot for shot, both shooting rounds of 68 on day one, 70 on day two, and 65 on day three, leaving the rest of the field far behind.

Although Nicklaus began day four with two birdies to pull ahead, Watson fought back and, after 16 holes in the final round, the pair were still level. Then Watson birdied the par-five 17th to take the lead for the first time. A spellbound gallery watched as Watson's drive found the fairway on the par-four 18th while Nicklaus's drive ran into the rough on the right. Watson hit a seven-iron to within five feet to set up a birdie, while Nicklaus played a fine recovery shot from the long grass to lie 11m (12yd) from the pin. Playing, as Peter Ryde wrote in The Times, 'with the courage of despair', Nicklaus miraculously holed his birdie putt, but an implacable Watson, needing the birdie, calmly rolled in his five-footer for a championship record of 268 and his second Open title.

Watson went on to become the world's top golfer soon after this victory at Turnberry, as did Australian Greg Norman after he won his first Major – the 1986 Open Championship at Turnberry. Eight years later, Zimbabwean Nick Price, the dominant golfer of the early 1990s, laid to rest the ghosts of his missed opportunity at Royal Troon in 1982 when he finished eagle-birdie-par at Turnberry to edge out Swede Jesper Parnevik and claim the Claret Jug.

The most recent hosting of the Open Championship at Turnberry, in 2009, was one that nearly became the most famous story in all of golf and would have marked a fairytale ending to the illustrious career of one of golf's favourite sons, Tom Watson. On Sunday afternoon, 59 year-old Watson had an eight-foot putt for par on the 18th to claim his sixth British Open and a myriad of records, including the oldest ever winner of a major championship (beating Nicklaus' record by 13 years). What could have been the greatest Open victory in its history was sadly not meant to be, when he missed the putt and plummeted out of the four-hole playoff to effectively hand the Claret Jug to the deserving American Stewart Cink.

Although devastated at the thought of what could have been, Watson has been honoured for his time at Turnberry with a commemorative plaque erected on the 18th fairway. In preparation for the 2012 Senior British Open held here, the plaque details the 161m (178 yd) 7 iron that Watson hit from the fairway to within two feet of the pin. Watson sunk the putt to claim the 1977 British Open from Jack Nicklaus by a single stroke.

Turnberry's Open winners have been golfers reaching the pinnacle of their abilities and, as such, they are fitting champions for one of Scotland's most outstanding golf courses.

ROYAL BIRKDALE
LANCASHIRE, ENGLAND

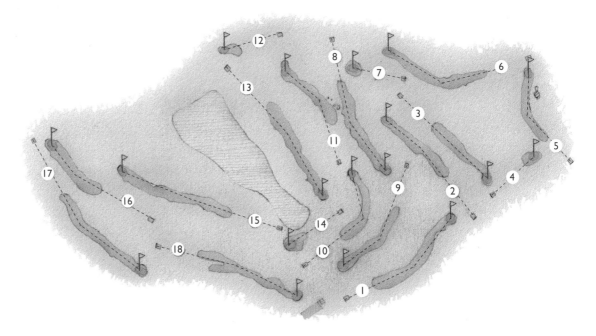

FAR RIGHT: A new 12th hole, nestling among rolling sand hills, was constructed at Royal Birkdale in 1965, the year in which the course hosted both the Ryder Cup and the Open Championship – which was won by Australian Peter Thomson.

Royal Birkdale, on England's Lancashire coast, has hosted over 31 championships and international matches since World War II, making it the most important tournament venue in England. Most recently, it played host to the 2008 Open Championship won by Ireland's Padraig Harrington. The 137th open was remembered for its wild weather, with a constant wind that didn't drop below 32 Km/h (20mph) for the entire tournament. Padraig won by a convincing four strokes to claim the first major of his incredible year.

Birkdale has a history of worthy Open champions. Peter Thomson won his (and Birkdale's) first Open in 1954 and it was also here, in 1965, that the Australian held up the Claret Jug for the fifth and final time. In 1961, American Arnold Palmer powered his way to victory at Royal Birkdale after playing what is undoubtedly his most famous shot. On what was then the 15th hole – it is now the 16th – Palmer drove the ball into the rough, where it came to rest under a bush 135m (150yd) from the green. He seemed set to drop a shot but, in an astonishing display of brute strength, he played a six-iron out of the bush, over the bunkers and onto the green. The shot is commemorated by a plaque in the rough at the 16th, marked by a rose bush.

In 1971, Mexican Lee Trevino was a popular winner of the 100th Championship when he

beat Taiwan's Lu Liang Huan (or 'Mr Lu' as he was affectionately known by the crowds at Birkdale). It was Trevino's third victory in 23 days, following his success in both the US and Canadian Opens.

Although American Johnny Miller managed, in 1976, to overtake three-day leader Seve Ballesteros to claim victory, it was the young Spaniard who dominated the headlines during that week at Birkdale, which effectively launched his career. The 1983 Open saw another five-time winner, American Tom Watson, lift the Claret Jug, while in 1991 a relatively unknown Australian, Ian Baker-Finch, held off the challenges of Mark O'Meara and Ballesteros to clinch victory – a golden moment in a career that has never again reached such heights.

First opened in 1889, Royal Birkdale was a nine-hole layout just over a kilometre from the current 18 holes. Eight years later, George Lowe from neighbouring Royal Lytham & St Annes was brought in to oversee construction of the new Birkdale course. The layout has seen several revisions over its long history. In 1932, FG Hawtree and former Open champion JH Taylor remodelled the course to turn Birkdale into a tough championship course. They threaded the fairways through the valleys between the giant, scrub-covered sand hills rather than over the top of them, thus avoiding the undulating fairways and blind tee shots typical of links courses. It was also

at this time that the new clubhouse was constructed, with wide windows looking out over the course towards the Irish Sea.

Maintaining the family connection, FG Hawtree's son, Fred, was brought in to remodel the course again in 1963 and, in 1991, following complaints about the greens during that year's Open, a third generation of Hawtrees was called upon. Golf course architect Martin Hawtree, son of Fred and grandson of FG Hawtree, was given the task of reconstructing Birkdale's greens. He created what is rated as one of the fairest championship courses, with only one blind tee shot – at the 9th hole.

Unusually, the course is made up of three loops, with the 9th, 14th and 18th greens situated near the clubhouse. Before the 1998 Championship, further changes were made. Most notably, 6000 white pines were removed from the course with a view to restoring the links feel of the layout. In addition, several holes were made longer, pushing the length of the course off the championship tees to a challenging 6417m (7018yd).

With this new, open layout ideal for the viewing public, and its length and exposure to the sea winds ensuring that it is kept tougher than ever for the players, Birkdale seems set to maintain its position on the championship roster well into the 21st century, with the course set to host the Senior British Open in 2013.

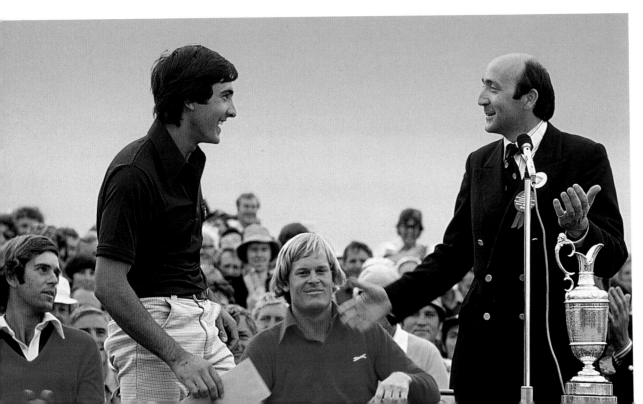

ABOVE: Royal Birkdale's fairways are laid out in the valleys between scrub and gorse-covered sand hills.

LEFT: A young Seve Ballesteros of Spain (left) accepts the runner-up cheque while winner Johnny Miller of the USA waits to receive the Claret Jug after winning his first and only Open Championship at Royal Birkdale in 1976. Ballesteros went on to win the event in 1979 at Royal Lytham & St Annes, in 1984 at St Andrews and for the last time in 1988, again at Royal Lytham & St Annes.

MEDINAH

ILLINOIS, USA

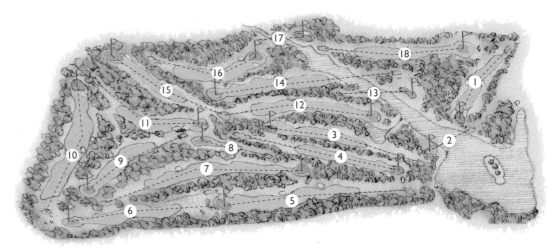

S ituated in a suburb of Chicago, Medinah was built in the 1920s for the Ancient Arabic Order of Nobles of the Mystic Shrine, a society known for its charitable works.

Scottish architect Tom Bendelow was commissioned to layout 54 holes on the 263ha (650 acres) of land west of Lake Michigan and, interestingly, the now-famous Course No 3 was originally constructed as the ladies' course. At just 5683m (6215yd) it was a far cry from today's extent of more than 7001m (7657yd).

The course was ultimately considered too difficult for ladies and was handed over to the men. When the 1930 US Open was played there, Harry Cooper roared through the final round on his way to a 63 and the title, more than a little irritating the members. As a result, five new holes were laid out to toughen it up and prevent similar feats in future.

Besides the length of Medinah, some 4200 trees make for a very unforgiving layout, placing a premium on exceptionally accurate driving of the ball. The course is laid out on 85ha (205 acres) of land, with only 12ha (30 acres) taken up by fairway. Add to this the notorious winds that whip off the lakes surrounding Chicago and it is no wonder that the USGA rates the par-72 layout at an enormous 77.1.

LEFT: At Medinah, tee shots are played across the long inlet from the expansive Lake Kadijah (named after Islamic Prophet Mohammed's wife) on no fewer than four occasions, including three par threes; the 2nd, the 13th and the 17th; and one par five, the long 14th.

ABOVE: The par-three 17th is played over the waters of Lake Kadijah from a raised tee down to a narrow green.

LEFT: *Built in the 1920s, the imposing clubhouse at Medinah has an intriguing blend of several architectural styles.*

Although Chicago is generally fairly flat, this is not true of the area on which Medinah is built. The holes, some of which are cleverly doglegged, rise and fall with the terrain, making club selection difficult, even without the wind. Although the greens themselves are fairly flat they are well guarded by some fiendish bunkering. Finally, water comes into play on three of the par threes, two of which measure over 183m (200yd) as well as the newly designed par four 15th . On the par-three 17th, the tee shot must carry all the way over Lake Kadijah (named after the wife of the Muslim prophet Mohammed).

Medinah's unusual clubhouse was built in the 1920s for an exorbitant US$600,000. With its unique architectural blend of Middle Eastern Byzantine, Louis XIV, Oriental and some Italian Renaissance elements, it includes a somewhat bizarre 18m (60ft) rotunda featuring spectacular mosaics.

Three US Open championships have been played at Medinah – in 1949 (won by Dr Cary Middlecoff), in 1975 (won by Lou Graham) and in 1990, when 45-year-old Hale Irwin had to play 91 holes to snatch victory, becoming the oldest-ever winner of the US Open. (Those were still the days of an 18-hole playoff, which Irwin took to an extra sudden-death hole against Mike Donald.)

Another Major, the PGA Championship, has been staged here twice and on both times has succumbed to the fearsome power of Tiger Woods. The first time was in 1999 when Tiger held off a spirited advance from young Spanish sensation, Sergio Garcia, to win his second Major title after his record-breaking victory in the 1997 US Masters.

When the PGA Championship returned to Medinah in 2006, world no.1 Woods came into the tournament as a hot favourite after his emotional British Open victory at Royal Liverpool and, in his usual fashion, obliterated the field by five strokes for a total of 18 under par 270. The victory was Tiger's 12th major championship and the second after the death of his father Earl.

The No.3 course at Medinah will also host the 2012 Ryder Cup, which inspired the club to undergo a significant restoration in 2009/10 that costed approximately $1.1 million dollars. Most notably, the par 4 15th hole has been shortened by more than 91m (100yd) to tempt the European and American teams into driving the green, although they risk losing the ball into the newly constructed two-acre lake on the right side of the hole.

The other major feature of the restoration included replacing 11 greens that were soil-based with new constructed sand-based greens, in order to conform to USGA standards. Holes 3, 4, 5, 6, 7, 8, 9, 10, 11, 12, and 14 were replaced, with the other 7 holes already having been rebuilt in 2002.

PORTMARNOCK

COUNTY DUBLIN, IRELAND

"I know of no greater finish in the world than that of the last five holes at Portmarnock."
Bernard Darwin

Situated across an estuary from Sutton in County Dublin, Ireland, the course at Portmarnock was set up by WC Pickeman and George Ross, who rowed across the estuary to the remote spot to construct it on the site of an earlier course – of sorts – owned by the Jameson family of Irish whiskey fame. Pickeman and a man named Mungo Park designed the first nine holes of the new course in 1894, with the other nine completed four years later. Yet another nine holes were laid out by Fred W Hawtree in 1970.

Naturally, the course is accessible by road today, but when Pickeman and Ross made the journey it was by ferry, about which there are many legends. One recounts the story of the intolerant club ferryman's disagreement with a passenger who was a clergyman of a different religious faith. Apparently, the ferryman refused to let him out at his destination, which was the Portmarnock course.

The course itself is typical of a links course, exposed to the elements, with weather that can change within the space of a few hours from sunny and benign to a howling storm. The original course was just some 5304m (5800yd) but, with advances in golf equipment, both clubs and balls, the championship course has since been extended to 6827m (7466yd). Of the 12 par fours, five are longer than 374m (410yd), while two of the three par fives measure well over 500m (550yd).

RIGHT: The par-five 6th hole, measuring 550m (605yd), is one of three par fives at Portmarnock that measure more than 475m (520yd). Scotland's Sandy Lyle set the course record of 64 at Portmarnock during the 1989 Irish Open.

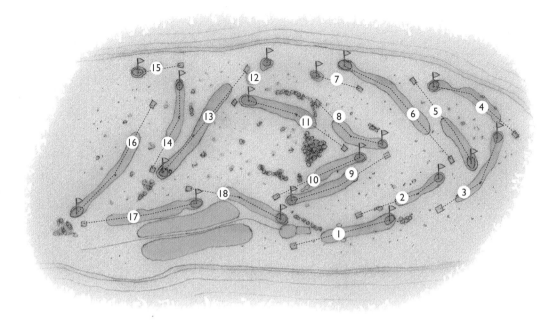

The course has played host to many important tournaments over the years, including the British Amateur Championship in 1949. Portmarnock has also been the venue for the Irish Open on 19 occasions, the most recent being in 2003 when New Zealander Michael Campbell posted an 11 under par total of 277 to win Ireland's national championship, just two years before he would win the US Open.

The course's signature hole is probably the par-four 14th that runs towards the Irish Sea. It has a deep bunker on the left of the fairway to catch wayward drives as well as a series of bunkers that guard the small raised green. This is followed by the spectacular 186m (204yd) par-three 15th that runs parallel to the beach. It is said that successfully negotiating these two holes is critical to achieve a respectable score at Portmarnock.

Because it has no hidden challenges, Portmarnock is considered to be an honest test of skill without reliance on modern design trickeries and was rated by Golf Magazine as #46 in the Top 100 Courses In The World in 2011.

ABOVE: The par-three 15th at Portmarnock is one of several holes that border the Irish Sea and is consequently exposed and vulnerable to the constantly changing weather conditions – a tough handful even for the professionals.

SEMINOLE

FLORIDA, USA

I knew this was going to take some imagination and I think we've come up with something that is a masterpiece.'
-Gary Player '

As the game of golf boomed throughout the USA in the 1920s, the era became known as the Golden Age of golf course architecture. In 1929, the great Donald Ross created Seminole Golf Club on the coast of Florida. Born in 1872 in Dornoch, Scotland, Ross was later appointed as professional and greenkeeper on one of the country's great links courses, Royal Dornoch. After emigrating to the USA in 1899, he worked at the famous Pinehurst golf resort in Massachusetts where he was to remain as director of golf until his death in 1948.

Raised on linksland courses, Ross incorporated many Scottish-style features into his layouts. This is apparent in the open, links-like landscape at Seminole, which has extensive bunkering and many water hazards, while the natural contours of the land have been left in place and trees are scarce.

Although significant modifications were made by Dick Wilson in 1947, and again by Ed Connor in 1991, the course retains its distinctive Ross character. Many holes at Seminole are designed to play alongside the ocean, including the signature hole, the par-four 18th. A stunning finishing hole, the fairway follows the beach leading up to a narrow green, which undulates heavily towards the greenside bunker on the right. The terrain of Seminole is mostly flat, although most of the tees and undulating Tifdwarf grass greens are slightly elevated, and a ridge of mounding comes into play in the middle of the golf course.

Florida is a golfer's paradise with a vast number of golf courses, so it is some commendation for Seminole to be rated as the top course in the state by Golf Digest in 2011-2012. This 18-hole, par-73 course, playing to 6535m (7,147yd) and rated 73.6 off the back tees, was also ranked #23 in Golf Magazine's Top 100 Courses In The World in 2011.

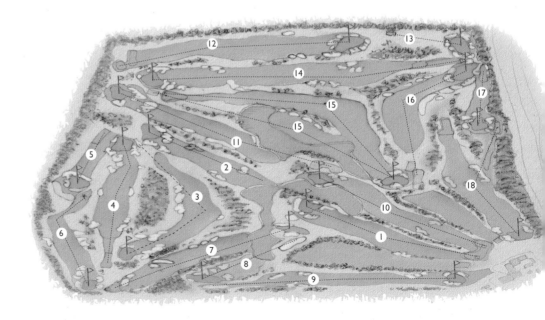

FAR RIGHT: The par-four 7th at the Links at Fancourt. The flat farmland on which the course was built was once used as an airstrip.

CARNOUSTIE

ANGUS, SCOTLAND

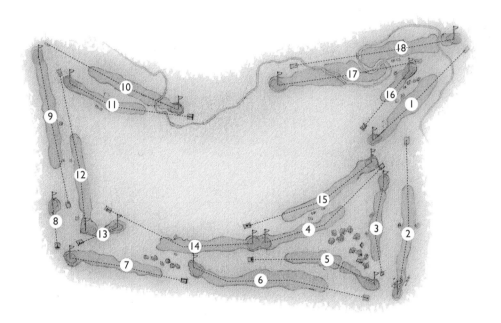

RIGHT: The 155m (168yd) par-three 13th is protected by a large bean-shaped bunker in front of the green.

Regarded as the toughest links course anywhere, the monster that is Carnoustie lies on the linksland near the Tay estuary on the east coast of Scotland.

The first 10 holes were laid out in about 1840 by Allan Robertson, with the final eight holes being the work of the legendary Old Tom Morris around 1857. James Braid, one of the famous 'Triumvirate', together with JH Taylor and Harry Vardon, was commissioned to revamp the course in 1926, some five years before the Open Championship was played there for the first time.

The course is brutally long at over 6700m (7300yd) and is made even tougher by the winds that whip off the sea. No more than two consecutive holes head in the same direction, so the player has to cope with the wind from all angles, while two fast streams, Jockie's

Burn and the infamous Barry Burn, also meander their way through the course.

The Open Championship has been played at Carnoustie seven times since 1931, when Tommy Armour won.

In 1953 Ben Hogan entered the Open for the first (and only) time, arriving at Carnoustie from the USA a full two weeks before the tournament began. From the first, he remained characteristically impassive towards the large, enthusiastic crowds he drew, earning himself the uncomplimentary nickname of 'the wee ice-mon'. In gale-force winds and intermittent rain, Hogan produced a clinical display of golf, eventually finishing with a four-round total of 282, the second-lowest total in Open Championship history at that time. It was not until 1968 that the Open was again played at Carnoustie,

LEFT: A view back down the 18th fairway showing the notorious Barry Burn which crosses the fairway short of the green.

when Gary Player was the one to triumph. Then, in 1975, Tom Watson won the first of his five Open Championships.

For 24 years Carnoustie was ignored as a venue for the Open, mainly because of its lack of accommodation facilities and therefore its inability to cope with the huge influx of players, officials and spectators. With the building of the stunning new hotel overlooking the 18th green, many of these problems have been solved and 1999 saw Carnoustie return as an Open venue.

The 1999 Open will be forever remembered for two things. Firstly, the rough was allowed to grow punitively thick and the fairways were as narrow as 13.7m (15yd) in places. Scores ballooned and vociferous criticism of the farcical nature of the course setup was rampant. Spanish teenage sensation Sergio Garcia's reputation took a knock when he opened with an 89 in the first round, following with an 83 for a two-round total of 172, missing the cut by 20 shots.

Secondly, it will be remembered for the spectacular collapse of Frenchman Jean van de Velde who blew a three-shot lead on the final hole, his ball finding a watery grave in the Barry Burn on the 18th hole – proving that water need only be a few metres wide to be a devastatingly effective design feature. Little-known Scotsman Paul Lawrie went on to win the four-hole playoff against van de Velde and

American Justin Leonard, to record his first Major victory.

After 1999 it only took eight years for the Open to return to Carnoustie, when Ireland's Padraig Harrington recorded his breakthrough major championship victory here in 2007. Ironically, the last time a European had won a major was the eventful 1999 Open and the last time an Irishman had lifted the Claret Jug was in 1947.

Harrington nearly repeated the infamy of Jean Van de Velde's undoing when he stuck his drive into the Barry Burn and made double-bogey to force a four-hole playoff with Spain's Sergio Garcia. With both players vying for their first major victory, Harrington succeeded in beating Garcia by a single shot and narrowly avoided joining the ranks of those who have let the Claret Jug slip away on the 72nd hole.

Carnousite is also a resident course that hosts one of the rounds of the Alfred Dunhill Links Championship, and in the same year it hosted The Open a course record 64 was shot by Australian Peter O'Malley in round two.

Recently, Carnoustie hosted the 2010 Senior British Open won by Germany's Bernhard Langer and was honoured as #21 in Golf Magazine's Top 100 Courses In The World in 2011.

ROYAL ST GEORGE'S

KENT, ENGLAND

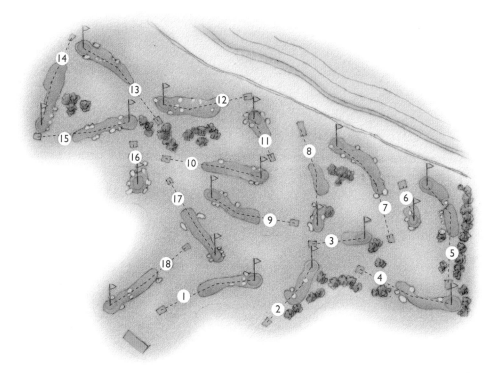

Royal St George's is one of England's greatest and most historic links golf courses, hosting the first ever Open Championship to be played in England as well as on 13 subsequent occasions. The first tournament in 1894 also saw the first victory by an Englishman, JH Taylor, marking the start of the domination of this event by Taylor, James Braid and Harry Vardon, who became known as the Great Triumvirate.

Royal St George's was clearly a course to Taylor's liking, as he went on to become the first man to break 70 in an Open here in 1904. Between them, the Great Triumvirate won 16 of a total of 21 Open Championships played between 1894 and 1914.

Vardon recorded two of these victories at Royal St George's, while the great Walter Hagen won two of his four Open titles here, in 1922 and 1928. The course was also the scene of South African Bobby Locke's victory in 1949.

RIGHT: The green of Royal St George's par-three 16th is surrounded by bunkers, requiring an accurate tee shot, particularly when played into the prevailing wind. This links course has hosted the Open Championship for over a century, JH Taylor winning the first in 1894.

ABOVE: A thatched starter's hut and a bell post flank the 1st tee at Royal St George's. A short drive at this hole will leave the golfer with a difficult long second shot to be played out of the hollow known as 'The Kitchen'.

RIGHT: Ireland's Harry Bradshaw came close to an Open Championship victory at Royal St George's in 1949. He tied with South Africa's Bobby Locke after 72 holes of regulation play, having carded a double-bogey six on the 5th after playing the infamous 'bottle shot'.

The first British Open Royal St George's hosted in the new millennium was the 2003 Open Championship, where third-round leader Thomas Bjorn joined Open infamy by blowing his two shot lead on the 16th hole to give the Claret Jug to American Ben Curtis.

More recently, in 2011 Northern Irish veteran Darren Clarke lifted the Claret Jug after beginning the tournament with his odds winning at 200-1. Beginning the final round with a one shot lead over big hitting American Dustin Johnson, Clarke held off challenges from Rickie Fowler and Phil Mickelson to cruise into a five under par total of 275, three shots clear of Johnson. In a post win interview, Clarke expressed his sentiment for The Open:

"The Open to me is the oldest, the biggest, the best there is. There's nothing more than The Open."

Situated among towering sand hills overlooking Pegwell Bay in southern England, Royal St George's was built by Dr Laidlaw Purves, a Scot who had moved down from Edinburgh in the 1880s. Inland golf courses were not highly regarded at that time, and Purves was looking for a suitable seaside site to construct a Scottish-style links course for London golfers. Regarding the piece of land near the village of Sandwich as perfect, he formed the Sandwich Golfing Association in 1887 and proceeded to lay out a golf course. Despite the occasional modification over the years, the course today remains essentially true to the original layout.

Playing to a par of 70, Royal St George's measures 6587m (7204yd) off the back tees and is characterized by undulating fairways that often result in the ball coming to rest on a slope. Sea breezes off the bay add to the challenge.

Royal St George's is perhaps best remembered for what has become known as the 'bottle shot'. During the 1949 Open Championship, Ireland's Harry Bradshaw was at the top of the leader-board during the final round when he played his approach shot to the par-four 5th. His ball came to rest inside a broken beer bottle behind the green. According to the Rules of Golf, Bradshaw would have been allowed to take a free drop, which probably would have seen him putting for par. However, unaware of this particular rule, he chose to play the ball as it lay, smashing it out of the bottle and eventually carding a double-bogey six. At the end of regulation play, he found himself tied on 283 with Bobby Locke, who then went on to beat him in the playoff.

ROYAL TROON

AYRSHIRE, SCOTLAND

R oyal Troon, on the west coast of Scotland, is recognized as one of the toughest courses on the British Open roster. The prevailing wind is from the northwest and, as is typical in many links courses, the holes follow a nine-out and nine-back layout. This means that golfers set out with the wind at their backs, but are faced with the full force of the Ayrshire weather on the homeward journey, making this long course (6561m; 7175yd) an exceptionally stern test.

Golf was first played over this piece of land as early as 1870, but it was not until 1878 that the club was established. The present layout has been influenced by several notable course architects: the 1883 Open champion, Willie Fernie, made various alterations to the layout during his tenure as club professional, while James Braid, Dr Alister Mackenzie and Frank Penninck also made significant contributions.

For many years, Troon boasted both the longest and shortest holes in Open Championship golf. What was once the longest, the 6th is a fearsome par five at 549m (601yd). Even in favourable conditions, it is difficult to reach the green in two, and when the wind is blowing it is downright impossible. The shortest hole is the 123m (134yd) par-three 8th. Sometimes it may require no more than a wedge to find the green but, if the wind comes up off the Firth of Clyde, it may demand as much as a three-iron. The hole is called the 'Postage Stamp' because of the size of its green, but the saying goes that unlike a normal postage stamp, this one is not easily licked.

It is best remembered for two contrasting incidents. During the 1950 Open, German amateur Hermann Tissies took 15 on this hole, although he only had one putt. His tee shot found one of the 'Postage Stamp' green's five deep bunkers. He needed five strokes to escape, only to find a similarly difficult bunker on the opposite side of the small green. Another five strokes saw him return to the original bunker, from where he required another three to escape, before one-putting for 15.

LEFT: Royal Troon's par-five 6th is named Turnberry. At 527m (577yd) it is one of the longest holes encountered on the Open rota. The landing area off the tee is guarded by a triangle of cavernous bunkers, while the green is long, narrow and raised.

RIGHT: Royal Troon's par-three 8th, the so-called 'Postage Stamp', is at 115m (126yd) the shortest hole in Open Championship golf. The tiny green is surrounded by five yawning bunkers, and a very uncertain lie awaits in long grass low to the right of the green.

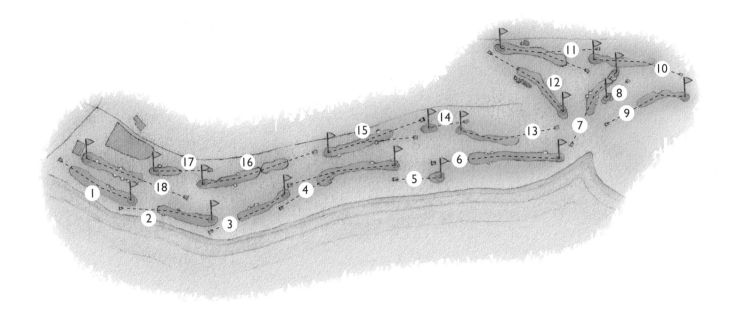

American Gene Sarazen played in his first British Open in 1923, which was also the year Troon first hosted the event. Although Sarazen was the reigning US Open and US PGA champion, he failed to make the cut at Troon after a bout of typical Ayrshire coast weather saw his day-two score balloon to 85.

Half a century later, on the 50th anniversary of the first Open at Troon, Sarazen – who had gone on to become the first player to take the Grand Slam of all four modern Majors – was invited to participate in the 1973 Open Championship. Then 71, he played his tee shot at the 'Postage Stamp' on day one with a five-iron: the ball pitched just short of the hole and rolled in for a hole-in-one. The following day, Sarazen again played a five-iron, but found a greenside bunker. The man who had invented the sand wedge climbed down to play his recovery shot – and it went straight into the hole for a remarkable birdie! Although he went on to miss the cut in the event, the memory of those shots will live forever. Sarazen presented his five-iron to the Royal & Ancient Golf Club of St Andrews, where it is still on display today.

Royal Troon has hosted the Open on eight occasions. Arthur Havers won the first event in 1923, and a host of illustrious golfers have since gone on to win here. In 1950, South African Bobby Locke won with a score of 279, the first time 280 had been broken in the tournament's history, and defending champion Arnold Palmer set a record score of 276 in 1962. Tom Weiskopf equalled Palmer's score to win in 1973, while Tom Watson collected the fourth of his five Open titles at Royal Troon in 1982. American Mark Calcavecchia held off Australian Greg Norman and Wayne Grady in the Open's first four-hole playoff in 1989, while American Justin Leonard was a gracious and popular victor in 1997.

The most recent Open hosted by Royal Troon was in 2004 and displayed the rollercoaster final round The Open has become known for. Going into the final round with a one shot lead, American Todd Hamilton experienced fierce challenges from Ernie Els and Phil Mickelson. Playing in the final group with Hamilton, Els stole the lead and on the final hole had a birdie putt to seal victory, but instead missed and was forced into a four-hole playoff with Hamilton. Calm and collected, Hamilton made four pars on his way to lifting the Claret Jug for his first major championship victory.

Royal Troon was named #48 in Golf Magazine's Top 100 Courses In The World.

WINGED FOOT

NEW YORK, USA

In the early 1920s, AW Tillinghast was instructed by members of the New York Athletic Club to construct two 'man-sized' 18-hole golf courses at Mamaroneck, New York. Tillinghast, one of America's great golf course architects and the designer of the renowned Baltusrol Golf Club in nearby New Jersey, cleared 7800 trees and moved 7200 tonnes of rock, eventually creating the Winged Foot East and West courses that opened for play in 1923.

While the East course is considered to be more attractive, the West course is regarded as a true championship test, playing 229m (250yd) longer, at 6642m (7264yd) off the back tees.

It has hosted the US PGA Championship once and the US Open four times. For America's national championship, the par-72 layout (rated 73.5) is made considerably tougher by converting the par-five 9th and 16th into par fours to play to a total par of 70. Ten of the course's 12 par fours measure over 366m (400yd) and, although the layout undoubtedly favours the longer hitter, its 60 bunkers – including at least two deep bunkers near every green – also put a premium on accuracy. All the greens, raised and subtly contoured, are constructed in Tillinghast's trademark pear shape.

In 1929, professional golfers from around the country came to

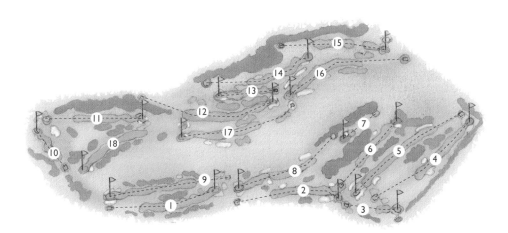

Left: The green of Winged Foot's par-five 12th hole is elevated and pear-shaped, a feature that is a trademark of renowned course designer AW Tillinghast, who built the course in 1923.
ABOVE Gary Player, pictured playing at Winged Foot during the 1974 US Open, earned the nickname 'the Black Knight' as a result of his golfing attire.

LEFT: American Davis Love III sinks the winning putt on the 18th green at Winged Foot to take the 1997 US PGA Championship and lift the coveted Wanamaker Trophy. The victory marked Love's first-ever win in a Major championship.

Winged Foot to examine Tillinghast's creation and participate in the first US Open hosted there. The great Bobby Jones, already the winner of two US Opens and undoubtedly the favourite, pleased the crowds by tearing up the course on day one with a superb 69. However, his 75 the following day provided a dose of Winged Foot reality and, at the end of 72 holes of regulation play, Jones was tied for the lead with Al Espinosa on 294, requiring them to return for the customary 36-hole playoff. Jones, who had previously lost two US Opens in playoffs, did not falter on this occasion, opening with a solid 72 while Espinosa,
unaccustomed to the pressure, shot an embarrassing 84. Jones closed with another brilliant 69 to win the playoff by a staggering 23 strokes and take his third US Open title.

The US Open returned to Winged Foot in 1959 when Billy Casper was the winner, while Hale Irwin was victorious in 1974 with a seven-over-par total of 287, and Fuzzy Zoeller defeated Greg Norman in a playoff in 1984.

In 2006, Winged Foot's most recent hosting of the US Open, Geoff Ogilvy's winning total of five over par 285 represented the brutality of the layout and the dynamic nature of the Open itself. With a two shot lead heading into the 16th hole, Phil Mickelson unravelled as he made bogey and a double bogey on the last to relinquish the trophy. The Open wasn't exactly handed to Ogilvy either, as he had to chip in for par at the 17th and sink an eight-foot par putt on the 72nd hole to win his first major.

In 1997 Winged Foot was chosen to host the year's final Major and the course's first US PGA Championship. Immensely talented golfer Davis Love III finally put to rest the 'best player never to have won a Major' tag with a convincing victory over Justin Leonard.

While Winged Foot Golf Club's affiliation with the New York Athletic Club has long since ended, the club has always retained the winged foot logo – and this challenging layout remains a 'man-sized' test, even for today's big-hitters.

ROYAL ADELAIDE

ADELAIDE, AUSTRALIA

"One finds a most delightful combination of sand dunes and fir trees, a most unusual combination even at the best seaside courses. No seaside courses that I have seen possess such magnificent sand craters as those at Royal Adelaide."
-Dr Alister MacKenzie

ABOVE: 7TH HOLE: The 167m (182yd) par three hole features some amazing bunkering.
BELOW: 8TH HOLE: the long, hourglass-shaped tee of the par four 8th hole.

The location of the Royal Adelaide Golf Club has moved several times since the club was founded in June 1870. After beginning on a course prepared on the North Parklands, the club dappled with several locations before finally purchasing real estate near Grange in 1904 and the 'Seaton' links were officially opened on the 30th of June, 1906. It wasn't until 1923, however, that the club was granted permission to use the prefix 'Royal', which has remained in the title ever since.

Royal Adelaide is among the list of prominent Australian courses to have had architectural influence by the legendary Dr Alister MacKenzie, who toured the country in 1926. Perhaps this is the reason for Royal Adelaide being ranked continually in Australia's top five, and for its proximity to the top 50 courses in the world.

The Dr's visit saw a significant, yet welcomed, change to the layout as the sand dunes that once surrounded the course were incorporated into the links as a natural hazard. Utilizing the native character of the landscape was an architectural trend Dr. MacKenzie was renowned for and one that reflected the early Scottish links courses.

This philosophy is encapsulated in the short par four third hole, in which MacKenzie used the sand dune as the ultimate risk/reward scenario. At the blind tee shot, the golfer must choose whether to take on the sand dune to drive the green or to play up to the crest of the dune for a likely par. Falling short of either one of these options faces heavy punishment and can puzzle amateurs and tour players alike.

In the last 30 years more changes have been made to the holes on the periphery; their original, flat designs have been landscaped to give a more challenging and undulating test of golf. The current layout stands at 6634m (7258yd) and was ranked #85 in Golf Magazine's Top 100 Courses In The World in 2011.

Royal Adelaide has hosted nine Australian Open Championships; the previous occasion was in 2006 when Australians Michael Sim and Paul Sheehan enthralled audiences with a two-hole play-off, Sheehan claiming the victory on the second extra hole. In addition, pop-sensation Justin Timberlake was seen playing the Seaton links in 2007 whilst on his Future Sex/Love Show tour in 2007.

NEW SOUTH WALES

SYDNEY, AUSTRALIA

"It's one of the great golf courses I've seen, really a fun golf course. You could have some real times out here."
Arnold Palmer – 27 Nov, 2004

Legendary golf course architect Dr. Alistair MacKenzie spent the last three months of 1926 touring Australia and acting as an architectural consultant to such courses as Royal Queensland, Manly, Royal Sydney, Royal Adelaide, Metropolitan, Kingston Heath and Barwon Heads.

But it was the spectacular NSW coastline at La Perouse that captured the doctor's imagination and led him to choose the eastern Sydney location as the site for the New South Wales Golf Club. So enthralled by the surroundings of La Perouse, Dr. MacKenzie claimed that with the exception of Cypress Point in southern California, this site would offer "more spectacular views than any other golf course in the world."

Although MacKenzie wrote the original Routing and Bunkering Plan in December 1926, it wasn't completed until Eric Apperly oversaw the necessary alterations to the course, according to his predecessors plan. Whilst it was MacKenzie who was responsible for the routing, it was Apperly who determined the bunkering of the course.

Apperly's contribution is believed to have made the NSWGC the masterpiece that it is today, having commissioned the restorations and lengthening required attaining Championship Status after World War II. The current Championship length of the course stands at 6245m (6829yd) and has a par of 72, although it rates 74. The highlight of Apperly's restorations is the internationally acclaimed par-three 6th hole. With the coastline sitting directly behind the green, this makes for one of the most breath-taking photos in all of golf once the sun begins to descend behind the Pacific Ocean.

The 5th hole is one the most magnificent par 5's in Australian golf. Originally, the tee was positioned on a sand dune to the left of its current location but during the World War II the Australian Army reclaimed the land, so the tee was moved inland and thus creating a blind tee shot over an enormous hill.

Once the golfer is over the rising slope, the fairway plunges down 30 metres towards the Pacific Ocean. The therapeutic scenery of a fairway walking down to a sea of breaking waves more than warrants New South Wales Golf Club's ranking of #34 in Golf Magazine's Top 100 Courses In The World in 2011.

LEFT: 7TH HOLE: The straight, uphill par four 7th hole is spectacular looking back from the green towards the rock on the Cape Banks peninsula.

TPC SAWGRASS

JACKSONVILLE, FLORIDA

The Tournament Player's Club (TPC) is a network of premier golf courses that were designed to be played by tour pro's and accommodate large crowds and as such make for outstanding venues for various USPGA Tour events. The dream to have a network of courses that encourage 'Stadium Golf' is the passion project of former USPGA Tour Commissioner Deane Beman, who had his idea come to fruition with the construction of the Stadium Course at TPC Sawgrass in 1982.

Iconic golf course architect Pete Dye worked with Beman to create a truly dynamic golf course, where each hole was so unique that no particular style of player had an advantage. The Stadium Course tests every player; with an even distribution of lengths, doglegs and is so intelligently routed that no consecutive holes run in the same direction, making wind judgment a major hazard.

Beman's vision of spectator golf is reflected in the annual The Player's Championship, which boasts one of the most elite fields on tour. Combine this level of golf with a picturesque course, excellent spectator infrastructure and high television ratings and it is no mystery as to why the TPC at Sawgrass has been dubbed 'the fifth major'.

The holes are designed to be strategic for the player and dramatic for the viewer and this harmony is encapsulated in the par 3 17th, nicknamed the 'Island Green'.

One of the most recognisable holes in all of golf, the 125m (137yd) 17th has brought many a champion to his knees by combining a short hole with an island green that leaves no margin for error.

For the spectators and audiences, the hole looks beautiful with the island green and they are treated to watching the world's best hit a nice, high iron-shot. But for the players, the 17th is something they try to ignore all day, only to have their hearts sink once they arrive at the tee. Some of the game's greatest players have reflected their thoughts on the 17th:

"Every course needs a hole that puckers your rear end." Johnny Miller, 1984.

"It is like having a 3 o'clock appointment for a root canal. You're thinking about it all morning and you feel bad all day." Mark Calcavecchia, 2009.

"It's fantastic because you know all day, you know 17 is coming. I think that's what makes the drama of this tournament and this course. " Adam Scott, 2005.

The championship tees extend the layout to measure 6597m (7215 yd) but a number of tees are available for the handicap golfer. The Stadium Course was ranked by Golf Digest as #41st in America's 100 Greatest Golf Courses for 2011-2012.

ABOVE: 17TH HOLE: The majestic 17th is one of the most recognizable holes in golf. Despite being a 'simple' pitching-wedge or 9-iron for the professionals, it can still undo a tournament leader in a heartbeat.

ABOVE: The clubhouse at TPC Sawgrass.

ABOVE: The 17th at TPC Sawgrass, from a different angle.

RIGHT: 16TH HOLE: Looking back down the fairway from the 16th green. The 478m (523yd) par five is a birdie opportunity before the player reaches the daunting 17th.

ROYAL LYTHAM AND ST ANNES

LANCASHIRE, ENGLAND

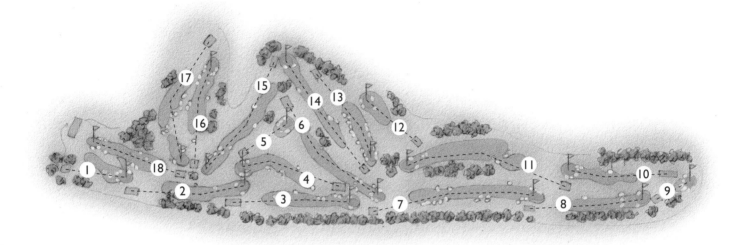

Royal Lytham & St Annes Golf Club is situated in Lytham St Annes, just outside Blackpool on England's west coast, bordering the Irish Sea.

Originally built (with an adjoining nine holes for ladies) on a piece of linksland leased from the St-Annes-on-Sea Land and Building Company in 1886, the club moved to its present site on the Fylde Coast in 1897. George Lowe is credited with the original course design, although course architects such as Harry Colt, Herbert Fowler and CK Cotton have had a hand in changes carried out over the years.

The substantial Victorian clubhouse was opened in 1898 after some 750 members raised what was then an enormous amount of £8500. It still stands today, overlooking the 18th green which is so close that in 1974 Gary Player was forced to play a third shot left-handed, using the back of his putter from against the wall after his approach ran through the green.

The course has been on the Open Championship roster since 1926 when Bobby Jones won the first of his three Open victories there.

Although now some distance from the sea, Royal Lytham has all the characteristics of a typical links course, with its links grasses, pot bunkers and undulating fairways and several blind tee shots. The course does not, however, run in the traditional links layout of the first nine heading outwards and the second nine returning in the opposite direction. The routing changes direction no fewer than 12 times. Additional oddities are that the round opens with a par three and there are back-to-back par fives at the 6th and 7th holes, while the back nine has only one par three and one par five.

At first sight, the layout seems fairly benign, but crosswinds can make judgement of distances extremely tricky. Royal Lytham & St

ABOVE: A view down the fairway of the par-four 18th at Royal Lytham & St Annes. The putting surface is situated within metres of the imposing Victorian clubhouse. To the left is the tee of the 1st, unusually a par three, and beyond, the Dormy House which offers accommodation.

Above: A plaque commemorates the astonishing shot on the 17th that enabled Bobby Jones to win the 1926 Open.

TOP LEFT: *Pot bunkers in the traditional manner litter the course, and every single green is strongly protected by them.*

BOTTOM LEFT: *Seve Ballesteros plays his tee shot at the short 9th during the 1988 Open Championship, which he went on to win in rather more conventional manner than he did in 1979, when his wild driving was rescued by miraculous recovery shots.*

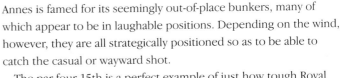

Annes is famed for its seemingly out-of-place bunkers, many of which appear to be in laughable positions. Depending on the wind, however, they are all strategically positioned so as to be able to catch the casual or wayward shot.

The par-four 15th is a perfect example of just how tough Royal Lytham can be. It measures a little over 430m (470yd) into the wind, and, for three days of the 1974 Open, the stroke average of the field was more than a shot over par.

The 6508m (7118yd) layout has now hosted the Open Championship on eleven occasions, on two of which the victor was a South African (Bobby Locke in 1952 and Gary Player in 1974). Australian star Peter Thomson won in 1958 and the New Zealand left-hander, Bob Charles, triumphed in 1963. In 1969, Tony Jacklin became the first Briton to win the Open in 18 years, and Seve Ballesteros won both in 1979 and 1988. In 1996, Tom Lehman became the first American professional to win the Open at Royal Lytham & St Annes, and was followed by compatriot David Duval in 2001.

Eleven years later, the Claret Jug arrived back at Royal Lytham for the 2012 Open Championship and for nearly 68 holes, it looked as though it belonged to Australian Adam Scott. Calm and collected all week, Scott began Sunday with a four shot lead and tragically joined the ranks of Open infamy when he bogeyed the last four holes to surrender his chance of a maiden major championship win. Playing in the group ahead, South African Ernie Els sunk an 18-foot birdie putt on the 18th to take the title away from his good friend but at least had these words of consolation:

"Sorry, you're a great player. You're going to win plenty of these."

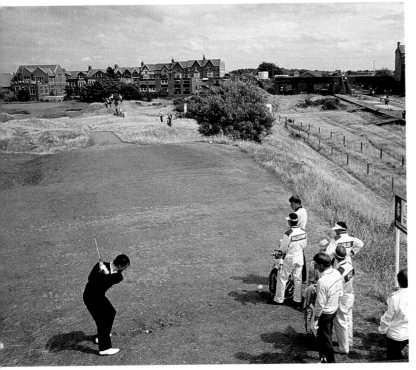

WENTWORTH

SURREY, ENGLAND

Wentworth in Surrey is widely regarded as one of the best inland courses in England. Construction began in 1923, on one of the first facilities in England based on the US country club idea, in which golf was not the only leisure activity available. It was also one of the earliest English developments in which houses were built alongside the fairways.

Two 18-hole courses and a short, nine-hole course were designed by renowned golf course architect Harry Colt. The shorter East course was completed first, followed by the West course in 1927. The West became the championship course and because of its length – it is now over 6677m (7302yd) – was nicknamed 'The Burma Road'. A third 18-hole course, called the Edinburgh, was added later, designed collaboratively by John Jacobs, Bernard Gallacher and Gary Player.

The West course, set among woodlands of firs and Silver Birch, underwent significant design changes by Ernie Els in 2006 to modernise its layout and it remains the venue for one of the world's most prestigious tournaments, the BMW PGA Championship.

ABOVE: Colin Montgomerie of Scotland, teeing off at Wentworth, where he has won the Volvo PGA Championship on three consecutive occasions from 1998 to 2000.

ABOVE: The scene at the green of the par-five 18th during tournament time. The West course is home to the annual PGA Championship as well as the World Matchplay.

RIGHT: An aerial view of the West course at Wentworth showing the par-four 11th hole on the left and the par-four 7th on the right.

Wentworth used to be the venue of the previously named HSBC World Matchplay Championship and was last held here in 2007, when course restorer Ernie Els claimed victory.

The PGA European Tour has its headquarters at Wentworth, so it is no surprise that one of its most prestigious tournaments, the BMW PGA Championship, is held here each May. All the big names take part and winners at Wentworth have included Bernhard Langer, Nick Faldo, Ian Woosnam, Colin Montgomerie and recent back-to-back winner Luke Donald (2011 & 2012).

With their extended television coverage, the closing holes at Wentworth have become extremely well known. The 17th is a long (557m/610yd) doglegging par five whose fairway slopes to the right while the hole curves through trees in the opposite direction. This makes a perfectly placed drive vital if the green is to be reached in two. The 18th, oddly enough also a par five, is substantially shorter at only some 492m (539yd), but its green is well guarded by large bunkers on either side.

Ending with two par fives has made for many exciting finishes in both matchplay and strokeplay events there, with players often 'going for broke' on those holes.

As it is not a links course, Wentworth will never be included on the roster of Open Championship courses, but it has hosted a match between the professionals of the USA versus those of Great Britain and Ireland (a forerunner to the Ryder Cup). In 1956, it also hosted the Canada Cup (now the World Cup).

ABOVE *The par-four 7th at the Links at Fancourt. The flat farmland on which the course was built was once used as an airstrip. Through the use of heavy duty earth-moving machinery, the Gary Player Design Group moved more than 700,000 metric tonnes of clay to create the natural-looking mounds and wetland features reminiscent of the great links courses of Scotland and Ireland. In describing the course, Gary Player has been quoted as saying, 'I knew this was going to take some imagination and I think we've come up with something that is a masterpiece.'*

FANCOURT

CAPE TOWN, SOUTH AFRICA

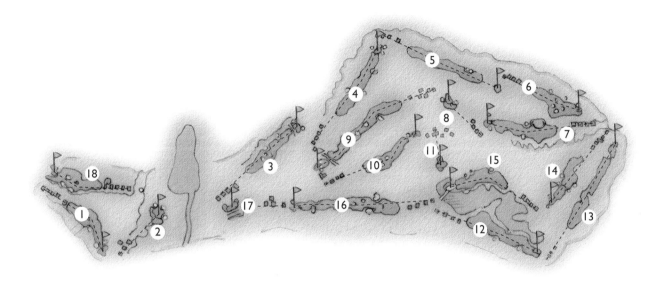

Fancourt Hotel and Country Club Estate in the small town of George is some 400km (250 miles) from Cape Town. Built as one of South Africa's first estate-type golf facilities in the early 1980s, it was saved from financial difficulties by German software magnate Hasso Plattner in the mid-1990s. Sparing no expense, Plattner commissioned a second course as well as a four-hole academy course and golf school, creating one of the finest estates in Southern Africa.

He then approached Gary Player, who had designed and constructed the first two courses, inviting him to construct a third world-class course – with a request this time to incorporate links-like characteristics.

Having studied courses such as Ballybunion in Ireland and other links courses in Scotland, Gary Player Design created a masterpiece on what had once been an airfield and later a dumping ground. Thousands of tonnes of clay were bulldozed to construct mounds on the flat ground to achieve the links-like effect.

The course has been designed to be the toughest test of golf in South Africa. As Gary Player has commented, golfers will realize that 'this game ain't meant to be fair!' Long and difficult, it is exposed to the winds that funnel through the impressive surrounding Outeniqua mountains and combines all the features of the best links courses of Scotland and Ireland: the long, secluded walks on fairways set between massive dunes; the waving Rye and Fescue grasses in the rough; and the blind and semi-blind tee shots and approach shots to large, undulating greens. Wetlands similar to those found on genuine linksland in the coastal regions of Scotland and Ireland have been constructed to add to the authenticity of the experience so that golfers in Africa can, as Gary Player desires, 'experience their very own British Open'.

ABOVE: *The approach to the par-four 3rd at the Links at Fancourt must be long enough to avoid the steep, banked 'burn-like' water hazard that crosses the fairway at the front of the green, another typical links-like feature incorporated into the Fancourt layout.*

Opened for play in November 2000, The Links at Fancourt is the only one of Fancourt's four courses open to non-members and non-residents of the estate or hotel.

In 2003, Fancourt hosted the prestigious President's Cup and delivered the hype leading up to the fierce rivalry. When The President's Team and The Internationals were tied on 17 points each at the end of the tournament, Tiger Woods (US) and Ernie Els (Int) entered into a sudden-death playoff. The two players halved three holes with pars on each and due to darkness the Cup was deemed a tie.

Most recently, Fancourt hosted the 2012 Volvo Golf Champions and saw veterans Ernie Els and Retief Goosen forced into a playoff with local talent Branden Grace. Only a week after claiming his first European title, 23 year-old Grace defeated two of his childhood idols when he birdied the first playoff hole.

NOORDWIJKSE

SOUTH HOLLAND, NETHERLANDS

The Noordwijkse Golf Club celebrated its 85th birthday in 1999, the year in which it hosted the 81st Dutch Open. The course on which this event was played, however, is slightly younger. In 1971 the old nine-hole course gave way to the expansion of the village of Noordwijk and the golf club was moved several kilometres to the north, where there was room for 18 holes and three practice holes. The layout at this location has rapidly built up an international reputation and established itself on the European championship roster. Exceptional patience is required to conquer this devilish course. Its typically links-like landscape of rolling dunes alongside the North Sea is made considerably tougher by the prevailing southwesterly wind. Designed by British golf course architect, Frank Pennink,

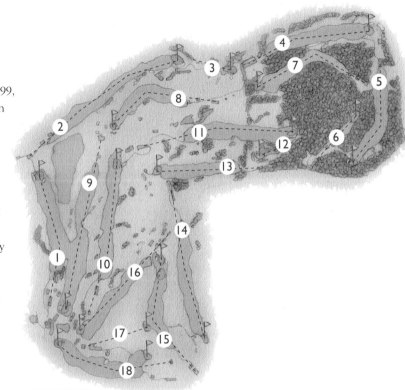

LEFT: The clubhouse at Noordwijkse Golf Club looks out over the green of the 9th hole.

ABOVE: The rolling dunes, open terrain and thick rough typical of links golf courses are apparent in this view of Noordwijk's 15th hole. The Dutch Open, traditionally played the week after the Open Championship, has been played at Noordwijk on nine occasions.

the 6317m (6908yd), par-72 layout has hosted the Dutch Open Championship nine times since 1978. Australian Stephen Leaney took the 2000 title with a 19-under-par score of 269. The following year, the newly named 'TNT Open' was held here and was won by the legendary Bernhard Langer with a 15 under par total of 269.

Spaniard Seve Ballesteros's victory in the Dutch Open played at Noordwijk in 1986 was remarkable for several reasons. He won by a runaway eight strokes, the same margin by which he won his first professional event – the Dutch Open at nearby Kennemer Golf Club – 10 years earlier. (Payne Stewart bettered this finish by recording a nine-stroke victory the next time the event was played at Noordwijk

in 1991.) Ballesteros's win in 1986 also made him the first European golfer to accumulate more than £1 million in prize money.

The 1986 event was, however, marred by the gouging of deep holes in the 3rd and 11th greens by anti-apartheid demonstrators, forcing PGA European Tour officials to take them out of play for one round. The record books show that Ballesteros's score of 271 was set over only 70 holes.

COUGAR POINT

SOUTH CAROLINA, USA

Kiawah Island, a strip of land 16km (10 miles) wide, off the coast of South Carolina in the USA, is rich in meandering lagoons and pristine marshlands. Bordered by the Atlantic Ocean to the south and the Kiawah River to the north, it is home to five exceptional golf courses.

The list of designers at Kiawah Island Resort reads like a who's who of modern golf course architecture: Pete Dye, Tom Fazio, Clyde Johnston, Jack Nicklaus and Gary Player – all names with a familiar ring – have each created a championship golf course in varied terrain of sandy dunes and forests of pine, oak and palm trees. The resultant collection of golf courses – Oak Point, Cougar Point, Turtle Point, Osprey Point and the Ocean Course – is as diverse as the architects themselves.

Cougar Point is Gary Player's creation on Kiawah Island, a 6286m (6875yd), par-71 layout featuring holes playing directly along broad expanses of tidal marsh and offering panoramic views of the Kiawah River and acres of needlerush and Spartina grass. Situated at the western edge of Kiawah Island, between West Beach Village and the river, the course

ABOVE: Appropriately in an area of lagoons and marshland, water comes into play on no less than 13 of the holes at Cougar Point, including the 17th, where Palmetto Palm trees line the back of the heavily bunkered green.

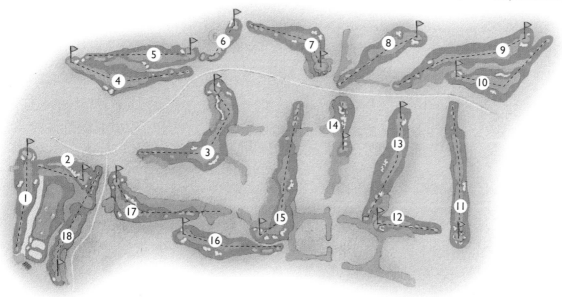

meanders through the island's marshlands where water is a prominent feature. In all, 13 holes have water hazards.

Cougar point cleverly caters for different styles of play as the long par fours feature wide fairways and running greens for the shorter hitter, whilst the short par fours place a high demand on accuracy off the tee for ideal angles into the greens.

The standout hole at Cougar Point is the par four 17th and is regarded as one of the most beautiful holes on Kiawah Island. With water following the whole right hand side of the fairway, golfers are tempted into a risk/reward scenario as the longer tee shots will make the approach to a well bunkered green easier.

Although the course is relatively short, it has small, undulating Tifdwarf Bermuda grass greens and its narrow fairways demand accurate shot placement. Cougar Point presents a challenge to the serious golfer, but the range of tee options allows even those with a high handicap to enjoy a social round.

ABOVE: Tall pines, oaks and palms line the fairways at Cougar Point, meandering through acres of waterways and swampland on the western part of Kiawah Island.

RIGHT: The green of the 5th hole at Cougar Point is situated on a raised peninsula surrounded by tidal marshland, with the Kiawah River visible in the background. Gary Player is one of five modern golf course architects to have created a championship course on Kiawah Island.

CONGRESSIONAL

MARYLAND, USA

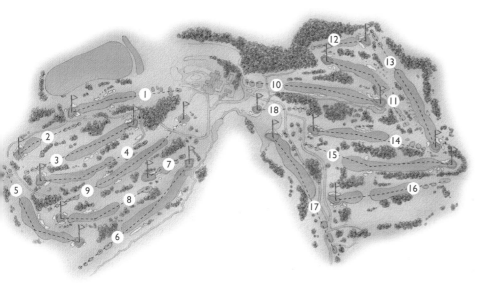

Ten kilometres north of Washington DC, in the rolling green hills of northern Maryland, lies Congressional Country Club with its lush parkland layout, tall trees and large expanses of water overlooked by a stately white clubhouse. Originally designed in 1922 by amateur golfer Devereaux Emmett after two congressmen decided to establish a country club on the 139ha (343 acres) of land, the course was officially opened by US President Calvin Coolidge in 1924. Secretary of Commerce Herbert Hoover was inaugurated as the club's first president, with luminaries such as Woodrow Wilson as founding life members.

The original golf course, which later became known as Congressional's 'Blue' course, served members of the private club well until 1957 when, with a view to attracting championship events to the course, Robert Trent Jones Snr laid out nine new holes of what was to become the 'Gold' course. His efforts were rewarded two years later when the US Golf Association (USGA) staged the Women's Amateur Championship there. Trent Jones also updated one of Emmett's original nines, making changes such as replacing the par-three finishing hole with a long par four. These improvements secured the US Open Championship for Congressional in 1964.

RIGHT: Congressional's par-three 7th features a narrow, tree-lined approach to a lightning-fast, sloping and undulating green.

LEFT: *Congressional is a long and demanding course. The 507m (554yd) par-five 15th hole requires two long and accurate shots for big hitters going for the green in two seeking a two-putt birdie.*

RIGHT: *Congressional's par-five 10th is played as a par four during the US Open. The course hosted the event most recently in 1997 when South Africa's Ernie Els beat Scotland's Colin Montgomerie by one stroke to claim his second Major title. A stream runs down the length of the right-hand side of the 10th fairway, feeding a pond alongside the deep, pear-shaped green.*

The 1964 US Open will long be remembered for the heroic performance of eventual winner, Ken Venturi. The layout that year measured over 6400m (7000yd), the longest course in US Open history, and two of the par fives had been converted to par fours. Back then, the last round of the US Open was played over 36 holes on the Saturday, the USGA believing 'endurance as well as skill shall be a requisite of a national champion'. On that Saturday morning in 1964, the golfers' endurance was severely tested in sweltering sunshine and high humidity.

Ken Venturi, not a physically strong man, finished the morning round in 66, although he faltered towards the end and was near collapse from heat stroke on the 18th hole. After rest and rehydration during the break, he was accompanied by a doctor and a thermos of iced tea as he set out for the second round – during which he carded an unforgettable 70 to claim the US Open title by four strokes.

In 1990, Rees Jones, the son of Robert Trent Jones, was called in to modify the course further, a father-son combination that resulted in the creation of a superb championship layout.

Congressional is a popular destination for USGA tournaments, having hosted the Kemper Open (later called the Booz Allen Classic) a total of eight times by big names such as Fred Couples, Greg Norman and Sergio Garcia. Most recently on tour, it has become the annual destination for the AT&T National, hosted by Tiger Woods who has won the 2009 and 2012 tournaments.

In the major championship arena, Congressional has hosted three US Open Championships and one USPGA Championship. Dave Stockton won his second PGA Championship here in 1976,

while in 1995 Tom Weiskopf edged out Jack Nicklaus to win the US Senior Open. In 1997, 27-year-old South African Ernie Els emerged on the Sunday from a four-man pack on the back nine to capture his second US Open title in four years. This was the first time the US Open had been played on the full 'Blue' course, as played by Congressional's members, with the championship ending on a 174m (190yd) par three – unusual for a Major championship.

However, with the USGA choosing Congressional as the annual host of the AT&T National and the 2011 US Open, the members were pressured by the governing body to change the course to avoid finishing on a par three. The USGA believed the final tee shot in a major championship needed to test the winner's ability to put the ball in a fairway, so the club voted to design a new par three for the 10th hole, and the routing altered so the 17th hole now plays as the 18th. The only inconvenience is a long walk from the new 10th green hole to the 11th tee.

With the alternations finalised, the new 6925m (7574yd), par 71 layout was ready to stage the second major of 2011. This was the third time Congressional had hosted the US Open and immediately it succumbed to the enormous talent of Northern Ireland's Rory McIlroy. Having surrendered the 54 hole lead of the US Masters in a disastrous fashion just two months earlier, 22 year-old McIlroy learned his lesson and put together the most dominant display of US Open golf in history. His 11 under par 36 hole score was the lowest in the 111-year history of the event, as was his final score of 13 under par and the eight shot lead secured his first major championship victory.

FIVE NATIONS

MEAN, BELGIUM

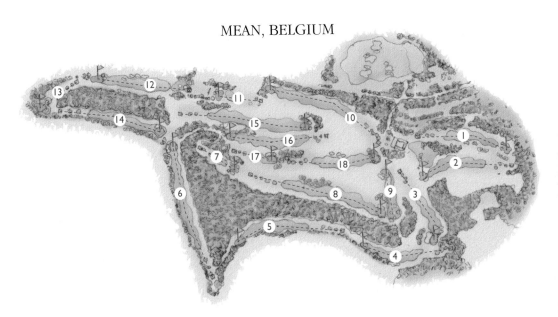

The Five Nations Country Club was created when a leading US property development company, Acquest International, sought to develop a truly international country club in western Europe. A suitable location within easy driving time of Belgium, Luxembourg, the Netherlands, France and Germany was targeted and, in 1988, a perfect property was found in the grounds of an existing golf course close to the Ardennes in Belgium. Here, Gary Player set about redesigning the course and clubhouse to international tournament standards.

The club is situated in the centre of the Brussels– Luxembourg–Bonn triangle, with these cities and their related international airports all within an hour's drive.
Set on 115ha (284 acres) of rolling, forested hills, the course features a number of holes that run along natural valleys, some of them bordered on the one side by a river and lined with woods on the other. This type of layout demands a golfer's utmost concentration and is a trademark of Gary Player's designs.

Although it is challenging, the 6038m (6603yd) course has multiple tee positions to enable golfers of all levels to excel, although the men's back tee has a par of 72. A significant elevation difference between the highest and lowest points on the course results in a number of holes playing dramatically downhill and provides for both exciting golf and magnificent panoramic views of the surrounding picturesque villages and chateaux. With its vantage points, the course is well suited for large spectator galleries, making it an ideal tournament venue.

The imposing clubhouse with its stone walls and cobbled courtyard is typical of the

ABOVE: *Five Nations Country Club is so named because of its proximity to four different European nations – Luxembourg, the Netherlands, France and Germany – from its location just south of Liège in Belgium.*

FAR LEFT: *The course at Five Nations was carved out of indigenous forest areas, utilizing existing streams as water features and hazards within the playing corridors.*

CHANTILLY

PARIS, FRANCE

Situated just 40km (25 miles) north of Paris, Chantilly is widely regarded as the finest course in France. Dating back to 1908, it has hosted the French Open Championship on more than 10 occasions, as well as other important events on the European golfing calendar. In 1913, Englishman George Duncan won the first French Open here with a total of 304 – still the highest winning total in the event's history.

After a break of some 14 years the French Open returned to Chantilly in 1988 when England's Nick Faldo triumphed with a four-round total of 274. The following year Faldo defended his title, again at Chantilly, bettering his four-round total by one shot.

Despite its woodland setting, the course itself is fairly open. However, punishing rough makes this 6597m (7214yd) course among the toughest in Europe. In the early 1920s,

Tom Simpson, who had redesigned parts of the Old Course at Ballybunion, was commissioned to redesign some of the holes that make up today's championship course. Ironically, considering the furore over the bunker that he added to Ballybunion, one of Simpson's major changes was to remove a number of bunkers. Although much of his work was badly damaged during World War II, the character imprinted by his changes is still in evidence today.

The course has three par fives and four uncompromising par threes, three of them more than 183m (200yd) long. Eight of the par fours are over 384m (420yd) long and have narrow fairways to add to the challenge facing the golfer. The 13th is particularly memorable, needing a solid long drive down the middle of the fairway to open up the approach to the green on this sharp dogleg left, before requiring a tough second

LEFT: The long par-four 11th features a two-tier green, making the approach shot critical if the player is to have a chance at birdie.

TOP: *Founded in 1909, Chantilly is an essential part of the history of golf in France. The Club House and the two 18 hole courses have become one of the monuments of international Golf. The final three holes start in front of the magnificent clubhouse. The 16th and 17th are played away to the end of the course.*

shot over a deep grassy hollow to a green surrounded by trees. Par on this hole is certainly a good score, especially in the midst of the pressure associated with tournament play.

The final three holes form a loop, taking play out and back from the clubhouse, the 16th another of those long par threes, and the 17th a solid, curving par four plentifully bunkered in the driving zone. The 18th, at nearly 550m (600yd), is an uncompromising par five that requires three well-struck shots to find the green and complete the round.

Chantilly is perhaps better known for its famous racecourse and equestrian centre, as well as the opulent Château de Chantilly and its art treasures.

Golf de Chantilly is consistently rated as one of Europe's premier golf courses and has recently been acknowledged as #12 in Golf World Magazine's Top 100 Courses In Europe in 2011 and #77 by Golf Digest in the Top 100 Golf Courses Outside The US in 2012.

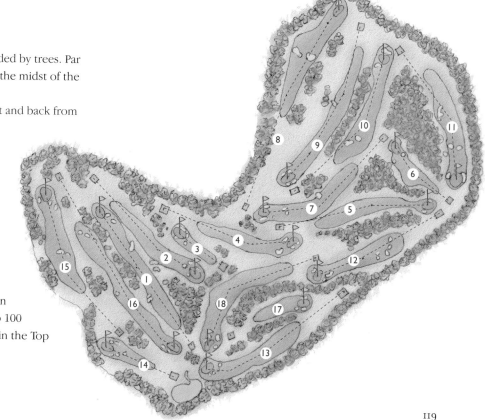

SPORTING CLUB BERLIN - NICK FALDO

BERLIN, GERMANY

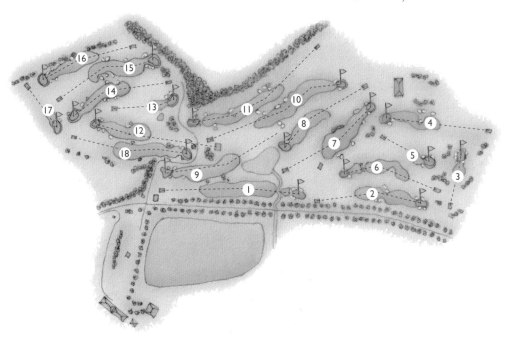

Three of golf's true masters, from three different nations, have each created an 18-hole championship golf course at the Kempinski Hotel Sporting Club near Berlin in Germany. The three are England's Nick Faldo, winner of six Majors, the USA's Arnold Palmer, winner of six Major titles and three Seniors Major titles, and Germany's own Bernhard Langer, twice a Masters champion.

Of the three layouts, it is the Nick Faldo course that is regarded as the best golf course in Germany and was recently rated #13 in Golf World Magazine's Top 100 Courses In Europe. Opened in 1996, it measures all of 6445m (7048yd) off the back tees and plays to a par of 72 although it is rated 74. It has already earned a place on the European championship roster, hosting the German Open in 1999 and the World Amateur Team Championship in 2000. Into his demanding layout, Faldo has incorporated elements of a Scottish links course in the form of deep pot bunkers, rolling fairways and high rough, all of which place a premium on placement. The course has grown rapidly in stature in Europe, with a leading golf publication ranking it among Europe's 10 best.

Opened in 1995, the exclusive Sporting Club Berlin on the picturesque lake, Scharmutzelsee, also offers tennis, horse riding and sailing to its members.

ABOVE: A view of the 9th green of the Nick Faldo course at Sporting Club Berlin. The course hosted the 1999 German Open, won by Sweden's Jarmo Sandelin.

SAN LORENZO

ALGARVE, PORTUGAL

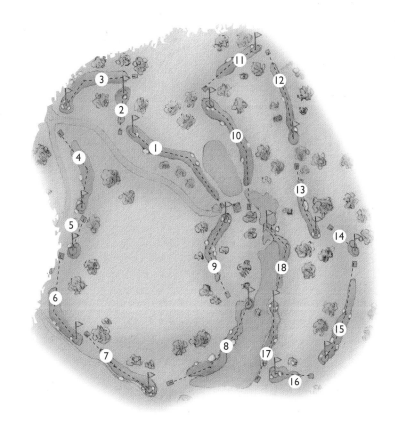

LEFT: San Lorenzo's par-four 6th hole offers spectacular views of the Ria Formosa nature reserve. Water runs along the right-hand side of the fairway all the way to the green. Similar views can be seen from the 7th and 8th holes as well.

BELOW: A large lake comes into play at San Lorenzo's finishing holes, the 17th and the formidable 18th. Tall umbrella pines line the course's perfectly manicured fairways.

Since the 2000ha (4942 acres) Quinta do Lago estate on Portugal's Algarve coast derives its name from the large number of lakes on this piece of land, water is a significant factor at the estate's San Lorenzo golf course. Designed in 1988 by American golf course architects Joseph Lee and Rocky Roquemore, San Lorenzo also features abundant umbrella pine trees and offers fine views over the woodlands and wildlife of the Ria Formosa nature reserve from the 6th, 7th and 8th holes which run alongside it.

The par-72 San Lorenzo layout, rated 73 and measuring 6238m (6822yd), features several holes that require tactical planning. Water laps the edge of the fairway all the way to the green on the spectacular par-four 6th, while the 8th is a 525m (574yd) par five leading up to a huge lake where a slice will lead to a dropped shot. The 18th is particularly dramatic, featuring an island green that demands a calculated, accurate approach.

The Algarve is a popular holiday spot and a well-known golfing destination, but for golfers aspiring to play San Lorenzo, money and a bag of clubs may not be enough. This busy public course is often booked up by residents of a nearby hotel and green-fee players sometimes struggle to get a slot.

The greenkeeper's policy of preparing San Lorenzo as if for a new tournament every day ensures that its superbly manicured condition is maintained and its status as the showpiece of the Algarve is secure.

RIA BINTAN

RIAU ISLAND, INDONESIA

The island of Bintan in Indonesia, just 45 minutes' ferry ride from Singapore's Tanah Merah Ferry Terminal, is home to one of Asia's most scenic ocean golf courses. The 27-hole Ria Bintan golf course meanders through serene tropical forest and along the South China Sea, providing golfers with breathtaking scenery and an exhilarating golfing experience. Apart from the course's striking natural elements, it is the bunkering that adds to its dramatic appeal. Sharp, steep faces, often cast in shadows, contrast with the white sand, luxuriously manicured greens, heavily wooded backdrops and churning sea.

Early in 1994, Keppel Land commissioned Gary Player to create a championship golf course. Player set to work on a piece of land he described as 'one of the best sites I have worked with anywhere in the world'.

The Ria Bintan golf course opened for play in late 1998, an important component of a 447ha (1105 acres) resort that is a joint venture between the governments of Singapore and Indonesia. It will eventually include various hotels, resort homes, seaside villas and condominiums, as well as a Club Med Holiday Resort.

The 6,470 m (7075yd) course's most spectacular hole is undoubtedly the par-three 9th, one of Asia's best short holes. The green is situated on a rocky outcrop that juts into the ocean, while cascading rocks have been used to form the platform for the green. Natural rainforest provides a backdrop to the long but very narrow putting surface – a distant target when the wind is blowing from the east. The 18th, a 445m (487yd) dogleg-left par four, with water to the left and dense forest to the right, is one of Asia's toughest finishing holes. A well-struck tee shot should find the generous landing area but the approach shot to the green must contend with a massive lake that extends right up to the putting surface.

RIGHT: Ria Bintan's 10th hole is a flat par four that doglegs left, following the coastline, to a large undulating green guarded by pot bunkers.

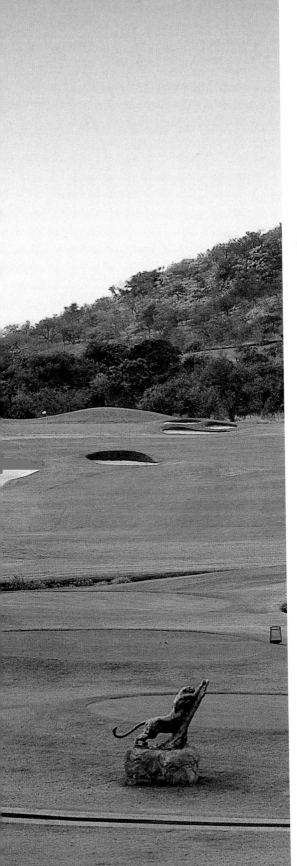

LEOPARD CREEK

MALELANE, SOUTH AFRICA

On the southern border of South Africa's Kruger National Park, near Malelane, is Leopard Creek Country Club, one of the country's most exclusive golf clubs. Business magnate and golfing benefactor, Johann Rupert, enlisted the skills of Gary Player in 1994 to construct what he envisaged as an 'African' Augusta. In a no-expense-spared project, Player was instructed simply to 'build the best course in Africa', which has indeed come to fruition as Golf Digest ranked Leopard Creek as number one in their Top 100 Golf Courses In South Africa in 2010 and again in 2012.

Rupert found in Player a kindred spirit: they share a deep love of golf as well as of the African bush. Completed in 1996, this golf course is magnificent in terms of the quality of the challenge it presents to golfers, the conditioning of the layout, and the way it blends with and enhances the natural environment. As it is set in the rugged wilderness of the Mpumalanga bushveld, sightings of crocodile, hippopotamus, wild pig, buffalo, elephant and various species of antelope are common, especially around the many watercourses and the Crocodile River that runs alongside three holes. The indigenous trees and bush on the course are also home to over 200 species of birds.

Creating and maintaining a championship-quality golf course in the middle of the African bushveld is no small task. Over 35ha (86 acres) of ground are under lush Kikuyu grass, but the original area had little topsoil and was covered in rock. A rock-picker was brought in to clear the land and 55,000m3 (1.9 million ft3) of topsoil were laid down to ensure a good base for the turf. Fine white bunker sand was trucked in from Bronkhorstspruit to cover the more than 1ha (2.5 acres) of bunkering, forming an attractive contrast with the green Kikuyu. To irrigate and maintain the grass, huge storage dams were constructed and an irrigation system was installed with over 1200 sprinkler heads, capable of pumping over three million litres (660,000 gal) of water a day onto the course.

Water features and dams form an integral part of the Leopard Creek layout, and the course's magnificent clubhouse looks out over the 9th and 18th greens, which share a common water hazard.

The peninsula green of the 9th hole is in fact completely surrounded by water, which is home to a number of hippos and crocodiles. The signature hole on the course is the 510m (558yd) par-five 4th. Situated on the banks of the Crocodile River, the green offers excellent views upriver where elephant can often be seen.

Virgin bush flanks the lush Kikuyu fairways, while stone walls and Scottish-style sod bunkers are a common fea-ture. Each tee is marked with a unique statue of a leopard, serving as a constant reminder that one is playing in the heart of the African bush.

LEFT: *The view down the 10th hole from the clubhouse at Leopard Creek shows the lush green fairways, which contrast strongly with the rugged African bushveld. A statue of a leopard marks the tee at each hole on the course.*

BELOW: *The 9th and 18th greens at Leopard Creek share a common water hazard, one that is home to a number of hippos and crocodiles. The fairways of these holes run parallel towards the greens situated in front of the magnificent thatched clubhouse.*

EMIRATES

DUBAI, UNITED ARAB EMIRATES

Situated just outside the thriving trading and holiday centre of Dubai in the United Arab Emirates, the Emirates Golf Club was the first all-grass golf course to be constructed in the deserts of the Middle East.

The brainchild of Sheikh Mohammed bin Rashid Al Maktoum of Dubai's ruling family, the championship Majlis course was opened for play in 1988. Designed by American Karl Litten, it measures around 6676m (7,301yd) and features many raised greens that add to its total length. The layout is generally tight requiring long, accurate tee shots, with the punishing rough made up of sandy desert and indigenous shrubs. The back nine features three par fives, two of which start or complete the loop. The par threes are fairly straightforward, while most of the par fours are taxing because of their length and awkward tee shots. As it is in the middle of the desert where daytime temperatures range from 30–49°C (89–120°F), nearly 4.5 million litres (990,000 gal) of water must be pumped on to the course through more than 500 sprinkler heads every day. An anomaly is that freshwater hazards on the course are plentiful, thanks mainly to the nearby aluminium factory with its adjoining water-desalination plant.

Emirates Golf Club is famous for its unique clubhouse, a towering construction designed in the shape of a Bedouin tent. Overlooking the 8th and 2nd greens, and 9th and 13th tees, is the similarly designed Royal Pavilion, the private entertainment centre for the Dubai ruling family's VIP guests at tournaments.

The Majlis course has hosted one of the European Tour's most elite events, the Dubai Desert Classic, every year (except for 1999 and 2000) since the tournament was created in 1989. The wealthy event has seen some of golf's greatest players claim victory and includes Seve Ballesteros, Mark O'Meara and Fred Couples to name a few. On the prestigious list of past champions, the most successful two have won it on more than one occasion. Ernie Els has won it three times (1994, 2002 and 2005) and Tiger Woods has won it twice (2006 and 2008).

Recently, the newly-named Omega Dubai Desert Classic has been dominated by Spain as Miguel Ángel Jiménez (2010), Álvaro Quirós (2011) and Rafael Cabrera-Bello (2012) have all claimed the winner's share of a $2.5 million Euro tournament purse. Majlis received further praise when it was honoured by Golf World Magazine in their Top 100 Courses In The World in 2011 and 2012.

In 1996 a second 18-hole course was added to the Majlis course at Emirates Golf Club. The 6701m (7328 yd) 'Wadi' course was designed by Nick Faldo and built around the perimeter of the original Majlis course. The course was named after the Arabic word for 'valley' and incorporates another three 'Academy' holes, a popular addition to the club's practice facilities.

Dubai itself has become the playground of the Middle East, catering to the surrounding Arab population as well as to visitors from further afield. It is as well known today for sporting events like horse and camel racing as it is for its shopping festivals.

ABOVE: *The greens of the 9th and 18th are overlooked by the luxurious clubhouse with its unique design inspired by the shapes of Bedouin tents.*

LEFT: *The holes on the Majlis championship course at Emirates Golf Club are typically surrounded by palm trees and many man-made bunkers. In the background can be seen the desert waste areas that line a few of the holes in stark contrast to the lush green of the fairways.*

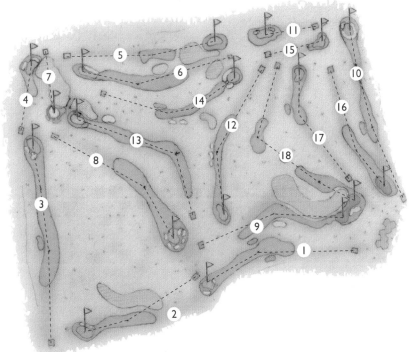

KAU SAI CHAU

HONG KONG, CHINA

Opened in 1995, the Kau Sai Chau Golf Course is one of only two public golf facilities in land-starved Hong Kong. In fact, there are two courses – the 6214m (6976yd) North and 5400m (5906yd) South – in a picturesque and tranquil setting on the northern end of Kau Sai Chau Island, with magnificent views of the Sai Kung hills on mainland Hong Kong.

Not surprisingly, neither of the Gary Player-designed courses is particularly long, and the greens and tees are fairly close to one another. As with most links-like courses, the winds off the surrounding sea play a dominant role, sub-stantially increasing the difficulty of both courses when they are at their fiercest.

The North course has several spectacular holes, including the par-three 3rd which is played across a water inlet to a steeply banked green. The undulating green means that even if a golfer successfully negotiates the 157m (172yd) distance, par is not a certainty.

The tee shot on the 425m (465yd) par-four 9th is across water to a wide plateau from which a long-iron is required to reach the green – and then only once the gusting winds that blow through a narrow valley at the rear of the green have been negotiated.

The par-four 15th is interesting for its walled fairway that creates a sheer drop on the left-hand side. The valley below is a breeding ground for a unique species of insects that were left undisturbed by the construction of the golf courses. The hole also has a panoramic view of the course, the imposing clubhouse and the sea in the distance. The par-five 17th makes use of a number of bunkers up the right-hand side of the fairway to force the tee shot to the left, a theme that is repeated all the way up to the green.

On the South course, the very short par-three 16th makes ingenious use of grass bunkers filled with waving Zoysia grass, requiring an accurate tee shot on a hole measuring just 98m (107yd).

Accessible by ferry from Sai Kung harbour, the course is open to anyone with an official handicap. There is also a 72-bay driving range and an academy, as well as several restaurants and other facilities like mini-golf.

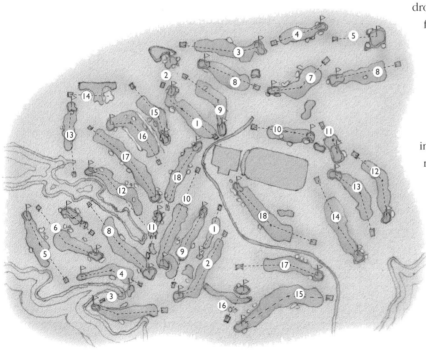

*LEFT AND ABOVE: The two 18-hole golf courses built on a former naval shooting range at Kau Sai Chau both feature typical links-like characteristics –
wide open rolling fairways, punishing rough and bunkers, and few, if any, trees.*

MISSION HILLS NORTH

CALIFORNIA, USA

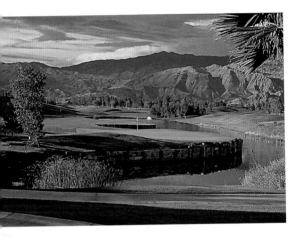

Under the wide blue skies of California, in the shadow of the barren and rocky mountains that tower over the dry plains of Palm Springs, lies the first Gary Player-designed desert golf course.

Player rose admirably to the unique challenges he encountered during the construction of this, his first desert course at the Westin Mission Hills Resort. Millions of dollars were spent sculpting the dry Palm Springs earth into an impressive landscape featuring lush Bermuda grass covering the fairways, tees and greens, as well as several lakes, four waterfalls and over 2500 trees, Oleanders and indigenous plants. Over 6000 tonnes of natural and artificial rock were used in the construction of the course's extensive water hazards.

Completed in 1992, the Mission Hills North golf course is one of two 18-hole layouts at the resort. Measuring 6458m (7062yd) off the back tees with a par of 72, Mission Hills North is a long course, and the use of extensive bunkering, multi-levelled or elevated greens, mounding, narrow fairways and water features on many holes make it a stern test. Nevertheless, the golfer is rewarded by a golf course that is both challenging and fair, with excellent views of the surrounding countryside.

The Westin Mission Hills Resort was named as one of Golf Magazine USA's Silver Medal Resorts in 1996. The magazine also ranked as a Top 75 Golf Resort by Golf Digest, a fitting tribute to Gary Player's vision, imagination and design skills.

ABOVE: Water plays a significant role at the Gary Player-designed Mission Hills North with lakes, streams and waterfalls coming into play on many of the holes.

RIGHT: Snowcapped peaks tower over the lush fairway and green of the 9th hole at Mission Hills North. This long par four is rated as the most difficult hole on the course. Mission Hills North hosts the LPGA's annual Nabisco Championship.

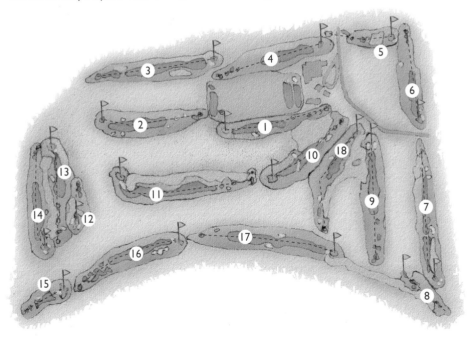

CAPE KIDNAPPERS

HAWKE'S BAY, NEW ZEALAND

Cape Kidnappers is one of golf's modern masterpieces and is an infant in comparison to rest of the golf courses in this book. But what this golf course lacks in age, it makes up for in the jaw-dropping beauty of its surrounds. Located on the eastern cliffs of New Zealand's North Island, the course was landscaped on the top of cliff fingers that sit 500 feet above the water of Hawke's Bay.

When American architect Tom Doak first saw the location of the sheep station at Cape Kidnappers, he saw an opportunity to construct a golf course on land that had been prepared for the sport by nature. Doak remarked that the sheep had trimmed the grass to fairway length so he was able to play 15 holes before anything had been constructed.

The initial holes of the course play away from the spectacular cliff tops until the golfer reaches the magnificent 5h hole, a highlight of the front nine as the cliffs welcome a hooked tee shot to the left and the fairway divides into two routes to the green.

The standout hole of the back nine is the par five 15th, which is routed along an enormous cliff finger that slopes down towards the water, where a cliff-side green awaits with the horizon behind it to punish severely any approach shots that are hit too long.

Whilst Cape Kidnappers was only completed in 2004, in just eight years, the 6510m (7119yd) par 71 layout has cemented itself in the elite golf courses of the world, having been ranked by Golf Magazine as #33 in the Top 100 Courses In The World in 2011 and an incredible #6 in Golf Digest's Top 100 Courses Outside America in 2012.

In 2008 and 2009 the PGA Tour chose Cape Kidnappers and Kauri Cliffs to be the host of the Kiwi Challenge. This PGA Tour Challenge event is played by four of the top PGA Tour players under the age of 30.

Cape Kidnappers is perhaps best known for its dramatic cliffside holes, but its inland holes — like the par-5 2nd holes — show off architect Tom Doak's dramatic bunkering and the terrain's distinctive heathland qualities.

LEFT: An early morning sun illuminates the a verdant, cliffside stretch of holes on the back nine (12-17) at Cape Kidnappers GC.

LEFT BELOW: The green at Pirate's Plank, the par-5 15th hole Cape Kidnappers, so named because the approach gives the impression of playing down a narrow corridor and finishing seemingly out above the South Pacific itself.

ABOVE: Aerial views of the back nine at Cape Kidnappers give a clear indication of the dramatic ravines and cliff tops that naturally shape the field of play.

CRANS-SUR-SIERRE

VALAIS, SWITZERLAND

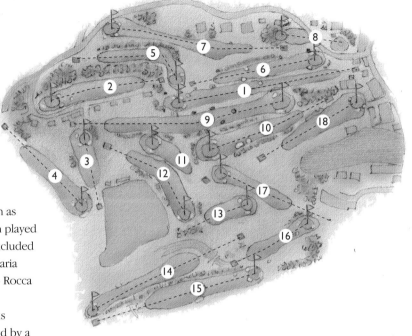

Crans-sur-Sierre, set high on a mountain plateau above the Rhône Valley in Switzerland's Berner Alps, must rank as one of the world's most spectacularly scenic golf courses. Each year in late August or early September, golfers on the European Tour gather in the shadow of the majestic, snow-capped peaks of the Alps and the rugged silhouette of the Matterhorn to play in one of Europe's oldest and most prestigious events: the Omega European Masters. Previously known as the Swiss Open and the Canon European Open, the event has been played here since 1939. Popular and worthy winners over the years have included the Spaniards Seve Ballesteros (in 1977, 1978 and 1989) and José Maria Olazábal (1986), Scot Colin Montgomerie (1996), Italian Costantino Rocca (1997) and Englishman Lee Westwood (1999).

Three-time winner Ballesteros is still fondly remembered for his miraculous recovery shot in the 1993 event, a feat commemorated by a plaque deep in the undergrowth near the 18th fairway. Ballesteros has a further interest in this golf course: together with the design team of his Trajectory Golf Course Design company, he has modified and redesigned all 18 holes at Crans-sur-Sierre.

Recent champion Thomas Bjorn (o symbol) of Denmark, was dubbed the 'King of the Mountain' when he shot a nine under par 62 in the final round to claim a four stroke victory of German Martin Kaymer.

Crans-sur-Sierre's altitude, 1600m (4390ft) above sea level, means that the 6165m (6744yd) par-71 course is shortened by the greater distances the ball flies in the rarefied air. This has allowed several European Tour records to be set here, most notably an 18-hole record of 60 by Italian Baldovino Dassu in the 1961 Swiss Open, and a nine-hole record of 27 by Olazábal in the 1978 Open.

Although skiing holiday pioneer Sir Arnold Lunn opened a golf course here in 1905, the sport did not prove popular among the region's tourists who preferred the pistes to the fairways, and it closed during World War I. The course was successfully reopened in 1927, and golf has grown in popularity in the area ever since, spurred by the hosting of the annual Swiss Open.

LEFT: The snowcapped peaks of the Swiss Alps form a spectacular backdrop to the green of the short par-four 7th hole at Crans-sur-Sierre. Above: Swiss-style chalets overlook the green of Crans-sur Sierre's par-four 4th hole. Measuring 456m (499yd), it is the longest and most demanding par four on the course.

KAURI CLIFFS

MATAURI BAY, NEW ZEALAND

ABOVE: A lone Norfolk Pine stands sentinel behind the 17th green at Kauri Cliffs GC, while the Pacific gently laps Pink Beach — also part of this massive 2500-hectare property — in the distance.

FAR RIGHT: Kauri Cliffs GC is located an aptly named community called Bay of Islands, near the northern tip of New Zealand. These are the Cavalli Islands that sit just offshore from the 16th putting surface.

Similar to the nearby Cape Kidnappers Golf Course, Kauri Cliffs is an astonishing piece of real estate where nature implies it was meant to be a golf course. When Wall Street financier Julian Robertson purchased the 4,000 acres of cattle ranch real estate on the majestic cliffs of the North Island's east coast, he would have wondered why someone had not developed a golf course here sooner.

Robertson soon employed American David Harman to design the course and the name was derived from the clusters of enormous native Kauri trees that sit atop the cliffs of Matauri Bay. With breathtaking views of the Cavalli Islands visible from nearly every hole, Kauri Cliffs was originally designed to be Robertson's own spectacular golfing retreat.

The integrity of this course lies in the intelligent design and is reflective of the philosophies of the great Dr. Alister MacKenzie; allow nature to dictate the routing of the course and incorporate the hazards around the natural topography. Harman used the sweeping summits, valleys, and gorges to create a challenging layout that winds down to the sea before taking the golfer into a valley at the beginning of the back nine. For a few holes the sea is out of sight but it returns at the 15th where the course gets closest to the cliffs.

A challenging layout, Kauri Cliffs offers severe penalties for shots off the wide, accommodating fairways and tough approach shots if played from the wrong driving lines. The standout hole is the 17th, where an elevated tee shot must be played over a valley to a fairway that runs down to a well-bunkered green. With the backdrop of the bay behind the green, it is the most picturesque approach shot on the course.

A well designed course atop one of the most beautiful settings in world golf, Kauri Cliffs is a must play for all golfers and was ranked #80 in Golf Magazine's Top 100 Golf Courses In The World.

ABOVE: Kauri Cliffs is famous for its seaside vistas, but the interior landscape is no less remarkable. Case in point: the stern-but-stunning par-3 5th hole.

INVERNESS

OHIO USA

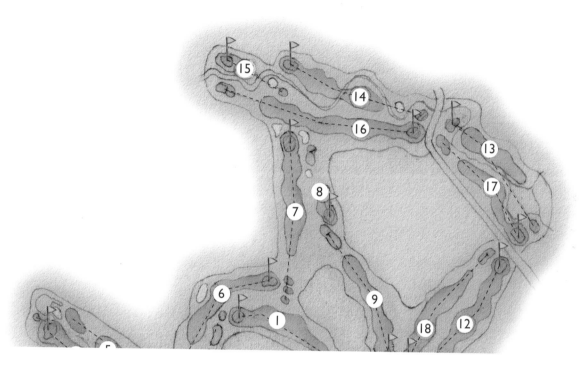

Professional golfers today are respected members of the golfing community, admired both for their ability on the golf course and for the standard of dress and decorum that has come to be associated with those in the paid ranks. However, in the early part of the 20th century, strong class distinction existed between elite, generally wealthy amateur golfers and professionals. This outdated tradition came to an end at the 1920 US Open at Inverness Club in Toledo, Ohio, when, for the first time, professional golfers were invited into the clubhouse, allowed access to the locker room and restaurant, and permitted to use the front door of the club. Inverness club president JP Jermain's gesture of hospitality was well received by the pros, particularly by two-time US Open winner Walter Hagen who presented the club with a chiming clock inscribed with the words:

'God measures men
by what they are

Not what they in wealth possess
That vibrant message chimes afar
The voice of Inverness.'

Pipe-smoking Englishman, Ted Ray, won the US Open that year, the first time the event had been staged at Inverness. Although the club opened in 1903, when nine holes were laid out through the wooded, gently undulating landscape, it was only in 1919, after18 new holes were designed by renowned Scottish golf course architect, Donald Ross, that it was elevated to championship status. Inverness hosted the US Open on three subsequent occasions, in 1931, 1957 and 1979, with modifications being made to the course before each event, first by AW Tillinghast, later by Dick Wilson, and finally by George Fazio. Inverness also hosted the US PGA Championship in 1986 and 1993, but it is for two particular incidents in its Major championship history that it is best remembered.

During the first round of the 1979 US Open, Lon Hinkle discovered a short cut to the green of the par-five 8th, the longest hole on the course measuring all of 483m (528yd). Hinkle's 'alternative route' involved deliberately hitting his ball off the tee onto the fairway of the adjacent 17th hole, from where he proceeded to birdie the 8th after knocking a full 55m (60yd) off its length. The organizers of the US Open, the US Golf Association, were so perturbed that, to the astonishment of the players, they planted a tall pine tree overnight, alongside the 8th tee to block the short cut. It measured 7m (24ft) in height and was 5m (16ft) wide at its base. Undeterred, Hinkle hit the ball over the tree and it became affectionately known as the 'Hinkle Tree'. That year the US Open was won by Hale Irwin, his second victory in the event. Behind him was 1965 US Open champion, Gary Player, who finished as runner-up in the event for the second time.

Inverness is a challenging golf course renowned for its lightning-fast greens and extensive bunkering: 110 sand traps dot the fairways and protect the greens. It was not until the 1986 US PGA Championship that par was broken in a four-day tournament over the 6284m (6982yd) layout.

That year, Bob Tway scored an eight-under-par total of 276 to record his first and only Major victory, but his performance is remembered for one superb shot. Measuring only 324m (354yd), the 18th is the course's shortest par four, but the small green is well protected front and left by several sand traps. Tway's approach shot found the bunker in front of the green, but his recovery shot landed softly on the green and rolled into the cup for birdie, giving him victory over Greg Norman. Coincidentally, Norman was again denied victory when Inverness hosted the 1993 US PGA Championship, with Paul Azinger defeating the Australian in a playoff to claim his only Major title.

Although Inverness has only three par threes and two par fives, which is unusual for a course chosen to host the US Open, the par-71 layout is rated 74.3 and, as a test of skill, it provides a fitting venue for the national championship of one of the world's great golfing nations. Inverness is continually ranked amongst the world's best layouts and was again named in Golf Magazine's Top 100 Courses In The World in 2011, at #71.

ABOVE: Inverness' par-four 5th green is surrounded by large sand traps. Extensive bunkering and lightning-fast greens characterize the Inverness layout, while, in typical parkland style, tall trees line the gently undulating fairways.

Above: Golfers make their way towards the final green from Inverness' 18th tee. Although this par four measures only 323m (354yd), designer Donald Ross laid several traps in front of, and to the left of, the small green to snare imprecise shots.

GARY PLAYER COUNTRY CLUB

SUN CITY, SOUTH AFRICA

ABOVE: South Africa's Ernie Els celebrates as his eagle putt drops on the par-five 9th hole during the 1999 Nedbank Golf Challenge. Els went on to win the event for the first time.

BELOW: The green of the par-three 16th at the Gary Player Country Club slopes sharply upwards from front to back, which varies the difficulty of the hole substantially depending on the chosen pin position.

FAR RIGHT: The spectacular island green of the par-five 9th at the Gary Player Country Club.

The Gary Player Country Club was the first course constructed at the famous Sun City resort in South Africa in the late 1970s. Although it is essentially a resort course, Player was given the brief to create a course that would test the very best golfers in the world in the Million Dollar Golf Challenge, now renamed the Nedbank Golf Challenge.

'What a golf course needs is elasticity, not simply to accommodate the long hitters, but in displaying a variety of tees with bunkers designed to challenge them,' says Player. 'Thus a golf course must be all things to all men. It must be flexible enough to provide a varying challenge for the old lady golfer, the young player and the top professional.'

Player introduced some of the most modern design features into the layout: large, clover-shaped and severely contoured greens, substantial mounds into which bunkers were cut, and multiple tee positions. The latter innovation, particularly, makes the course accessible to golfers of all skill levels. To the Nedbank Challenge pros, the course is a stern test, yet it presents plenty of birdie and eagle opportunities for those willing and able to rise to the 'risk and reward' challenge of Player's layout.

This philosophy is nowhere more apparent than at the par-five 9th, the course's signature hole. 'The 9th can be classified as a heroic par five, even though it is regularly set up to allow players to reach the green on their second shot. This is a hole where a swing of two or three shots can occur,' says Player. The hole has just one bunker – on the right and in the landing area of the tee shot. The fairway then curves left to a spectacular island green rising out of a dam with Sun City as a backdrop.

Golfers can play safe by laying up in front of the water and reaching the green in three; or they can attempt to reach the green in two for an eagle opportunity, but with a greater risk of putting it in the water.

The layout measures a daunting 7033m (7691yd) from the championship tees, providing a test worthy of the world's best, and the annual Nedbank Golf Challenge has grown to

become Southern Africa's biggest golfing event, televised around the world. The winners read like a who's who of world golf, including superstars Johnny Miller (who won the inaugural event in 1981), Seve Ballesteros, Bernhard Langer, Nick Faldo, Nick Price, Mark McNulty, Fulton Allem, Ernie Els and Colin Montgomerie. Keeping abreast of the huge influx of money into tournament golf, from 2000 the Nedbank Golf Challenge offers a generous $1.25 million to the winner. Lee Westwood has dominated the Nedbank Golf Challenge in recent years, winning the 2010 and 2011 events. Despite the length and difficulty of the course, Westwood has scored well in both victories with a 17 under par in 2010 and a 15 under par in 2011 and will try to make a hatrick at the even in November 2012.

The course constantly undergoes small design and construction changes to keep up with modern trends in golf course design and helped the club achieve #3 in Golf Digest's Top 100 Courses in South Africa in 2012. One is the bunker that has been added to the tough par-four finishing hole on the right of the fairway. The hole requires an accurate drive up the left side of the fairway but, because it is flanked by water, the right-hand side has always been the safe side. The hole then turns sharply to the left with the long-iron approach being played across water to a slightly raised green. The bunker now catches the conservative drive down the right, leaving the golfer a desperately

difficult shot to the green.

An important aspect of Gary Player's golf course design philosophy is that the course should enhance the environment. Only indigenous trees have been planted, the roads are dirt, natural stone has been used for retaining walls and walkways, and the rough bordering the fairways is thick, virgin bush.

Out on the course, far from the hustle and bustle of the resort and surrounded on all sides by tall trees and the peaks of the Pilanesberg hills that form the rim of an ancient volcanic crater, one can truly appreciate the tranquillity of African bushveld and the unique setting of this remarkable golf course.

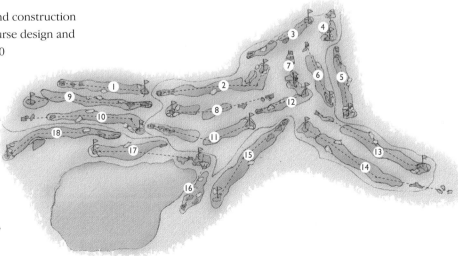

MANNA

CHIBA, JAPAN

The Gary Player-designed golf course at Manna Country Club near Chiba, east of Tokyo in Japan, is a parkland-style layout with the feel of a Japanese garden. Opened in October 1996, it is constructed on gently undulating land with tall, indigenous trees lining each hole. Its perfectly manicured fairways and tees, with greens of Zoysia Japonica and Bent grass, form a dramatic contrast with the white bunker sand and steep, brownish bunker faces, constructed from indigenous clay.

There are a number of streams on this 18-hole, championship-length layout measuring 6605m (7223yd) from the back tees. The signature hole is the scenic par-four 9th, which is 398m (435yd) long and has a stream running along the left side of the playing area.

The unusual clubhouse, designed in the style of an old European castle, was built of rock imported from the USA, while the luxurious interior was designed and finished by Italian craftsmen. The clubhouse also features a Gary Player Golf Academy and practice area, with a Japanese instructor certified to teach the Gary Player Method.

Japan has experienced burgeoning interest in the game of golf in recent years, and Gary Player has created no fewer than thirteen 18-hole golf courses in this country where land is at such a high premium. Manna Country Club has even constructed a second course with ageing Japanese citizens in mind. Among its attractions are eight health-check stations equipped with machines allowing golfers to measure heart rate and blood pressure, telephones in each booth so they can call a doctor in an emergency, and a monorail – complete with side platform for golf carts – to transport them from the clubhouse to the starting point.

LEFT AND ABOVE: The undulating terrain, scenic elevation changes, tall trees and an unusual bunkering style are typical of the Manna Country Club layout.

ABOVE: Note the steep,
brown clay bunker faces
which contrast with the
white bunker sand at
Manna.

VALDERRAMA

SOTOGRANDE, SPAIN

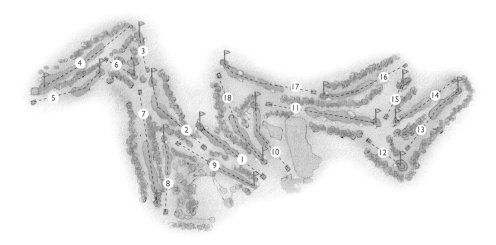

V alderrama is set among the rolling hills of the Sotogrande area of Spain's Costa del Sol. The course, originally called Los Aves, was laid out in 1975 by Robert Trent Jones Snr, who always considered it one of his finest creations.

Described as typically American, the course boasts many features supporting this characterization: vast teeing areas, massive greens with severe slopes, enormous bunkers and plenty of water.

Set among hundreds of cork trees on what was originally a Cork Oak plantation, the course does not demand great length off the tees, but a premium is placed on accuracy – both from the tee and in terms of 'placing' the ball on the correct section of the green with the approach shot.

In 1985 it was bought by a consortium headed by Spanish industrialist Jaime Ortiz-Patino, and Trent Jones was once again called in to revamp the layout. He tightened the driving line on several holes, placing greater emphasis on approach shots and generally toughening it up.

For some years Valderrama was the scene of the climax of the PGA European Tour's season, the late-season Volvo Masters. But in 1997 it acquired a greater international significance when it hosted the Ryder Cup, the first course in continental Europe to do so. Here Spanish golfing hero, Severiano Ballesteros, captained the European team to a single-

RIGHT: The green of the 500m (547yd) par-five 4th is protected by water all the way around the right half as the golfer approaches it.

point victory over an American team, which included the young Tiger Woods for the first time.

Ironically, it was Ballesteros who remodelled the 17th hole at Valderrama, easily the most controversial hole on the course. A par five, which at 467m (511yd) is easily reachable in two, it has two large humps in the middle of the fairway that can block off the approach to the green. As a well-struck, well-directed drive can be severely punished, it is felt that luck plays too great a part in a player's success on this penultimate hole.

In addition to the humps, the driving area is protected by fairway bunkers and the fairways incline sharply towards the distant water, making long-iron shots to the green extremely difficult. Layed-up shots can often trickle into the water short of the green as the slope takes the ball towards the water.

Once over the water, the green also slopes severely towards the water in front which means any ball with too much backspin can also find a watery grave. But then who said golf was meant to be fair?

In 1999 Valderrama became home to one of the US$5 million World Golf Championship tournaments that carry a first prize of US$1 million.

As the jewel in the golfers' paradise that is the Costa del Sol, Valderrama has become the model for other developments that continue to mushroom along Spain's idyllic south coast.

RIGHT: The approach to the green of the controversial par-five 17th showing the severe run-off into the water hazard from both the fairway and the green. The controversy centres on the contention that the large humps that block the approach to the green mean that luck plays too great a role in success or failure here.

RIGHT: Augusta National Golf Club, Hole 10

Photo Credit: Camellia

First published in 2012 by
New Holland Publishers Pty Ltd
London • Sydney • Cape Town • Auckland

Garfield House 86–88 Edgware Road London W2 2EA United Kingdom
1-66 Gibbes Street Chatswood NSW 2067 Australia
218 Lake Road Northcote Auckland New Zealand
Wembley Square First Floor Solan Road Gardens Cape Town 8001 South Africa

www.newhollandpublishers.com
www.newholland.com.au

A record of this book is available at the British Library and the National Library of Australia

ISBN 9781780093437

Publisher: Fiona Schultz
Project Manager: Alan Whiticker
Designer: Tracy Loughlin, Kimberley Pearce
Proofreader: Evin Priest
Cover photograph: New South Wales Golf Course, Sydney Australia
Production director: Olga Dementiev
Printer: Toppan Leefung Printing Ltd (China)

10 9 8 7 6 5 4 3 2 1

Keep up with New Holland Publishers on Facebook and Twitter http:--www.facebook.com-
NewHollandPublishers
Twitter: @NewHollandAU